A CATHOLIC JEWISH ENCOUNTER

A CATHOLIC JEWISH ENCOUNTER

Father Peter Stravinskas
&
Rabbi Leon Klenicki

Our Sunday Visitor Publishing Division
Our Sunday Visitor, Inc.
Huntington, Indiana 46750

Our Sunday Visitor Publishing Division
Our Sunday Visitor, Inc.
200 Noll Plaza
Huntington, Indiana 46750

International Standard Book Number: 0-87973-619-4
Library of Congress Catalog Card Number: 94-66023

Cover design by Monica Watts

PRINTED IN THE UNITED STATES OF AMERICA

619

Table of Contents

Preface

As we look toward the thirtieth anniversary of the
solemn close of the Second Vatican Council, our attention
is certainly focused on one of the most significant
developments resulting from that synod, namely the commitment of the Catholic Church to initiate and maintain a
conversation with the children of Abraham, to whom the
Roman Canon refers as "our father in faith." Decades ago,
people like Pope Pius XI and Jules Isaac noted the connec-
tions between Judaism and Christianity, but practical ap-
plication was often lacking on both sides for a variety of
reasons, which need not occupy us now. What matters is
that we are at a new and unique moment in the history of
the relationship between the Catholic Church and the
Jewish people.

This could not be highlighted in any more dramatic
manner than in the decision by the Holy See and the State
of Israel to establish formal diplomatic relations. In
Vatican II's *Nostra Aetate* (Declaration on the Relation of
the Church to Non-Christian Religions), we find the following observation and counsel: "Since Christians and
Jews have such a common spiritual heritage, this sacred
Council wishes to encourage and further mutual understanding and appreciation. This can be obtained, especially, by way of biblical and theological enquiry and through
friendly discussions" (n. 4). The work you are about to
read is a response to this call of the Council Fathers. Rabbi
Leon Klenicki and Father Peter Stravinskas, both men of

faith and personal friends for many years, combine theological scholarship with pastoral sensitivity, since both have labored in the academic world and also in congregations of their respective faith communities.

Those coming to this book expecting to find total agreement or even an attempt at a watered-down consensus will be disappointed, because these two authors have no intention of engaging in that kind of "false irenicism" already rejected by Vatican II's Decree on Ecumenism (n. 11). On the contrary, these two men clearly, cogently, and charitably present the authentic doctrine of their own faith commitments. Their conversation is an effort to produce understanding and, one hopes, ground for deeper reflection leading to an appreciation for convergences where they exist, as well as for differences in teaching or point of view. What I have described and what the authors have done, of course, is simply the task of dialogue — that process which brings about mutual understanding and respectful acceptance of the other as a brother or sister and a person of faith. As pastors and teachers, the authors have also provided readers with two important aids: a valuable glossary of theological terms in Judaism and Catholicism, and a guide for discussion at the local level, which might take place between churches and synagogues. What Our Sunday Visitor Books offers in this dialogue between a priest and a rabbi, then, is a paradigm for the dialogue which needs to occur at the grassroots.

One of the strengths of this book is that it examines themes that too often have not been present in Catholic-Jewish dialogue. The material here can easily lead groups to initiate dialogue on issues that will be helpful to explore together.

Having been involved in ecumenical and inter-religious affairs throughout the post-conciliar period, and being strongly committed to both until the present moment, I see a significant achievement in the writing and publication of this book which spans the terrain of theological discourse in a way which is at once accurate, interesting, and personal. And so, I applaud this effort of Rabbi Klenicki and Father Stravinskas, hoping and praying that their work bears fruit in the increased awareness of Jews and Catholics alike, indeed a heightened conviction, that "the gifts and the call of God are irrevocable. . . . To Him be glory forever. Amen" (Rom 11:29, 36).

Bernard Cardinal Law
Archbishop of Boston

Chapter One

Establishing the Rules

Background of the Dialogue

L.K. (Rabbi Leon Klenicki): We have been in conversation, Peter, for several years. I think that we started our friendship with a "disputation," disagreeing on certain matters of the Catholic League[1] and The ADLs'[2] position; I don't remember what the problem was in those days. But the good thing that came out of the discussion was our friendship. And the goodness of the interreligious dialogue is this reality of friendship itself — that a true interfaith dialogue means to know the other as a person of God and to feel the spiritual intimacy of the other. For this reason, we will discuss in our conversation aspects of the Christian-Jewish dialogue that are not usually taken into consideration.

Our main emphasis will be theological. Unfortunately, theology is not playing the role that it should play in interfaith dialogue; it should be central in the encounter of Jews and Christians.

P.S. (Father Peter Stravinskas): I'm delighted that our relationship has grown over time from probably a dozen years ago, when we first began our "disputation," as you called it. The very fact that we're able to be direct and honest with each other is an indicator of how far the dialogue has come. Sometimes Catholics have the impression that not much has happened in many of the dialogues

— not just the Jewish-Catholic dialogue — but all the various ecumenical dialogues with which the Catholic Church has been involved. There is a feeling that everything has reached a stalemate. But I think that our interest in having a sincere, heart-to-heart and head-to-head conversation is an indicator of where we are as two communities which indeed live under the sovereignty of Almighty God.

L.K.: We should start from the very beginning, that is, our youth. You and I have different youth experiences. I was born and raised in Argentina, and then came to study in the United States. The relationship of Jews with the Catholic Church in Argentina is quite different from the relationship between Jews and Catholics in the United States.

In my youth — my high school was a copy of the French lycée — we studied Latin and Greek and Western languages. We had courses in philosophy. I had very good teachers who were a remnant of the democratic "past," and new teachers designated by the Peronista regime. And that made a big difference, because some of the new teachers were right-wingers, in clear distinction to the other Catholics of the old regime, who were more open and much influenced by the thought of Jacques Maritain.

A philosophy teacher of mine introduced me to the thought of Maritain, and I was able to discuss with him and other students the main ideas of that French philosopher, whose thought was a real surprise after being exposed to the right-wing ideology of some fellow students and teachers. The fact of living in Argentina under a dictatorship has marked my life forever. I never experienced democracy until I came to Cincinnati to study to become a rabbi. It was a revelation for me to be able to talk openly on any matter, without any danger of losing a passport or being under police scrutiny.

I also appreciated religious freedom in the United States. I remember around Christmastime seeing on a wall in Cincinnati a billboard signed by a rabbi, the Archbishop of Cincinnati, and a Protestant pastor, asking everyone to pray for peace. I was so overwhelmed by that, that I wrote to my father about it, and I got an answer in a week or two, telling me that I should be careful: they might want to convert me. He was reflecting a reality different from what we knew in the United States.

P.S.: My background in terms of relations with the Jewish community is very different, not only because of being born and raised in the United States, but also as a function of the difference of our ages.

I was born in 1950 to parents of Eastern European background who were born in the United States. My understanding of Jews and Judaism was much conditioned by the background of my parents and grandparents. And that in itself is a kind of divided story. On both sides of the family, grandparents had negative images of Jews for whom they worked or whose tenants they were when they first came to the United States. Ironically enough, some of their closest friends were also Jews with whom or for whom they had worked, and with whom they had developed great personal relationships.

My father always had Jewish business partners, and so as a child I was quite accustomed to having Jews in our home. Most of them, I must say, were not very observant Jews, so certainly we were not much aware of kosher regulations. They themselves were very open to Christianity in general and to Catholicism in particular.

From the beginning, my formal religious education always presented me with extremely positive images of Judaism. I began kindergarten in a Catholic school in Newark in 1955; and the Sisters and the priests impressed on us the tremendous debt of Christianity, and specifically of Catholicism, to Judaism. At the opening of the Second Vatican Council, that positive understanding of Judaism was simply carried to its logical conclusion in my high school religion classes. I entered the seminary in 1968, which, of course, was just three years after the Council, and all of my priestly formation was influenced by these positive images as well.

L.K.: I would like to make a distinction between my Argentinean experience and my experience in the United States. I studied in Cincinnati at the Hebrew Union College and at the University of Cincinnati, where I got my philosophy and rabbinical degrees. At the University of Cincinnati, I wrote my thesis of philosophy on Saint John of the Cross. This created quite an uproar in my seminary, where one of the teachers asked me if I was going to write about the Gospel of John and whether I started to study Greek only in order to understand the text better. So I had to explain to him that I was going to write about a "John," but not necessarily the one of the Gospel. I read Saint John of the Cross when I was in high school in Argentina. Of course, it was a simple academic reading typical of a school, not projecting any spirituality. We read it because it was part of Spanish culture, in the same way that we read Saint Teresa of Avila. What I was interested in when writing about Saint John was a description of the technical-mystical language of the author. So, my thesis had a linguistic understanding, but also portrayed the spirituality of Saint John by his usage of the Spanish language. It is by chance, or not by chance — I leave that in God's hands — that at the time I was writing my thesis on Saint John of the Cross, a young Polish priest in Rome was writing his thesis on the same Spanish mystic. He became Pope John Paul II, and I'm just Rabbi Klenicki. I told that to the Pope some years ago. He embraced me and said that we were colleagues in Saint John of the Cross. What is interesting is that John Paul II wrote on the use of tradition by Saint John of the Cross, because the mystic was accused of abusing the tradition of the Church in his mystical consideration. Mine was only an attempt to understand the language that portrayed the spirituality of Saint John in his mystical experience.

Mutual Understandings

P.S.: I think that that's probably a good point of departure for us at this stage of the game, because first of all, if we ground ourselves in the whole question of spirituality and in our mutual understandings of God, then the rest of the dialogue has a good potential.

L.K.: At the outset let's discuss the main points of our religious commitment. One area of confusion in the Jewish community is its understanding of Christianity's conception of God as Trinity. In our monotheistic understanding (and that does not mean that the Trinity is not a monotheistic understanding), we experience God as the voice commanding us. By that I mean that God relates to the Jewish people through a covenant in which commandments are to be observed by the partner in this relationship, that is, the Jewish people. This makes "present" the presence of God for us.

P.S.: Certainly Christianity would have no difficulty with the understanding of God and the relationship of the community to God, as you have outlined it. When we talk about the trinitarian understanding of God, this is a very complex matter. Christianity over the centuries has had to walk a tightrope in this regard because there are various heresies that are possible, as you are well aware. The first four to five centuries of Christianity were plagued by heresies, both in regard to the identity of God as Three in One, and the place of Jesus in that Godhead. For example, one heresy was so intent on safeguarding the unity of the Divinity that God the Father was presented literally as the monarch of the Trinity and the role of Jesus was essentially reduced to that of an adopted son. In other heresies, the concept of Jesus' divinity was so stressed that it was unclear as to the differentiation of persons within the Trinity. So that's been a problem, not just for Jews on the outside trying to understand, but for Christians themselves. Of course, the classic explanation from Christian catechesis, not necessarily theology, is that of Saint Patrick, who used the example of the shamrock with three leaves in one plant, in order to demonstrate the unity and yet the diversity within the Trinity.

L.K.: In understanding the Trinity from a Jewish point of view, we have to realize that rabbinic Judaism has an appreciation for other dimensions of the personality of God. For example, the *shechinah* — the appearance of God present in moments of revelation or of communion with the people — can be considered as a second aspect or dimension in God's personality.

This highlights the fact that in today's atmosphere of theological relationship and interchange, we must be extremely careful with the language we use. Otherwise, we might commit all sorts of mistakes and misunderstandings, projecting into a word a dimension that does not belong to the word itself, from the perspective of the dialogue partner.

P.S.: I think that's a very important point to raise, Leon, and I've learned that even in dialogue with fundamentalist Christians. As you know, in the Catholic Tradition, we have a great devotion to Mary, and one of the titles that's accorded her is "Mother of God." To the untrained ear, that sounds at least blasphemous or mildly blasphemous. How could God have a mother? In fact, what we mean is that she is the Mother of God Incarnate. Within the Catholic community we can afford to be a little more casual, but when we're having a conversation with someone else, we must be sure the language does indeed reflect the reality in a precise manner.

A Question of Calling

L.K.: One point that requires our attention is the question of *election*. What does it mean that God would *elect* a specific group of people for a covenantal relationship? Let me refer to the first chapters of the Book of Genesis, which are important for the understanding of election in general, and of God's election of the Jewish people.

The first call of God is to Noah. This is part of our rabbinic understanding. It is a call and a covenant, because in rabbinic theology the triad Adam-Eve-God is not a covenant but a relationship. But in the case of Noah, it's the first covenant, a covenant of God with humanity. Jewish theology considers a covenant to be a relationship with a specific content, which is the moral law. Genesis Nine tells us of seven laws given to Noah to lead a holy life. Noah disregards that and falls into transgression. Now it is in Chapter Twelve that God issues a special call to Abram, who responds to God and accepts God's covenant. The result is the changing of his life and also of his name. Abram becomes Abraham and Sarai becomes Sarah, symbolizing the fact that the call of God changes the individual into a new person. This should be taken into consideration in our religious values, because many people take for granted the fact of living a religious life and accepting God as the everyday Partner of our existence.

P.S.: The whole concept of the call and the covenant with Noah is critical for setting the stage for Christian-Jewish dialogue, because there is obviously a great openness in Judaism to the possibility of a relationship of people with God beyond the formal borders of Judaism.

L.K.: One of our major thinkers, Eliahu Benamozegh, an Italian rabbi of the nineteenth century, wrote a very important book which I hope will be translated into English. His book is called *Israel and Humanity*, in which he discusses the question of Noah in relation to Christianity. For him, there is a connection between Noah and Jesus. Noah fails in his call to bring humanity to God. As we know from Genesis, he transgresses and is relieved of his task. Jesus, on the contrary, is the messenger of God to bring humanity to a covenantal relationship with the Eternal. This Jewish understanding of Christianity allows for a unique kind of dialogue, because it obligates us Jews to understand Christianity, not in historical terms of what it has done to Judaism, but as part of God's design to redeem the world.

P.S.: Yes, I found that notion helpful myself, but from the Christian side of the coin — namely, to appreciate the on-going value of the covenant with Israel, which has been a bone of contention in Jewish-Christian conversation. Thus, in some sense, we come to understand what Saint Paul talks about in the Epistle to the Romans: that indeed there is an ongoing relationship between God and the People of the Covenant — the covenant with Abraham, which is not abolished but perdures. Of course, then, the second question from a Christian perspective (which tends to want things nailed down a little more specifically than Judaism at times): How do Jews get saved if Jesus is *the* way to the Father, to God? How, indeed, can people other than Christians be saved? In Catholicism there is more of an openness to alternate routes to God and salvation than there might be in other forms of Christianity.

Salvation or Redemption?

L.K.: Peter, this is a very important point. First, the words that we are using. Can I talk of the concept of salvation in Jewish theology, and especially in rabbinic thought? I'm not so sure. I feel that the word that comes to our minds immediately is the word "redemption," understood as a process of improving the world by implementing God's commandments, thus bringing about the Kingdom of God on earth. God's commandments are basic in the Hebrew Bible, but they also need expounding. And that's what "*Halakhah*" (the body of Jewish law and tradition) has done through the centuries, and especially in the first centuries of the Common Era (CE).

When Jesus says, "I am the way," that expression is not problematic for me. It is very Jewish. Because Jesus was using the word "*Halakhah*," which can be translated as a "way of going." So, in that sense, I would accept Jesus as "the way." It is not my way, because as Franz Rosenzweig (one of the great Jewish theologians of our century) said, we Jews have been with the Father from the beginning. Perhaps the rest of humanity needs the Son to reach God. I have no problem about that. What concerns me is when I'm told that I might not be redeemed, or saved in Christian terms, unless I accept Jesus as the messianic realization.

Particularity and Saint Paul

P.S. If we look at Christian revelation, starting with Saint Paul, it's clear that Christian theology believes that the only way to salvation or redemption (the two are nearly synonymous in Catholic theology) is in and through the Person of Jesus Christ.

In some sense, we might refer to that as the scandal of particularity — how could it be? It's the same question raised, for example, by G.K. Chesterton (the great English convert and apologist of the early part of this century) as he spoke about the scandal of particularity in regard to the Jews. He asks, "Why did God choose the Jews?" And with all due respect and love, he suggests twenty-five reasons why God should have picked other people, humanly speaking, but as a matter of fact chose someone and some place and some time, and that's the scandal of particularity. The particularity of salvation from the Christian perspective is that it comes through Christ. But the question of how is very much up for discussion.

Saint Paul himself, in that famous eleventh chapter

of the Epistle to the Romans, really ends the meditation, which is a marvelous hymn to salvation from the Jews, by saying that ultimately this is in God's hands. I think when we try to pin God down to a specific timetable or plan of action, at that point we may be exhibiting a kind of a theological arrogance which goes beyond the scope of truly religious people. So I am quite content to maintain our doctrinal commitment to salvation in and through Jesus Christ, while at the same time saying that how God decides to work or has decided to work from all eternity in and through the Jewish people, and to save them as He saves all of humanity, is in some sense God's business.

L.K.: Peter, you referred to Saint Paul. I read Saint Paul when I was in Cincinnati. Dr. Samuel Sandmel of blessed memory was my teacher of New Testament, and a beloved friend. He asked me one day to read Romans Nine to Eleven for one of his classes, and afterwards I had to talk about my reading. My first comment was that I felt that Saint Paul was not a "simpatico" figure, due to my upbringing. I remember when I was a child my father used to say that "Jesus was a Jewish scholar, and a good human being. But what they did with him afterwards, it's a Christian business." But my father was very critical of Saint Paul. And I remember that once he caught me reading a novel on Saint Paul by Shalom Asch, a famous Yiddish writer. I devoured the book, and my father was upset that I was reading such a novel. But Asch was trying to show that, essentially, Paul was Jewish and was trying to bring humanity to God through Jesus.

I have been studying Romans Nine to Eleven for the last five years with great interest. I suspect that Paul projects a sort of ambiguity concerning the Jewish people that has become part of the Christian heritage. Sometimes one senses in Christian theology a sort of ambivalence towards the Jewish people and the Jewish vocation and mission. There's a recognition of the eternal call of God, and Paul says that God would not revoke a call, but at the same time there is an uneasiness about accepting Jesus and at the same time accepting the Jewish people as a partner of God. And this is the sort of ambiguity that we need to overcome in our conversation and in the careful study of Saint Paul. I consider Romans 9-11 central in the theological reconsideration of Jews and Christians together.

Ambiguity or Distrust?

P.S.: I agree with that completely. You talk about ambiguity, and perhaps we need to underscore the ambiguity that Jews feel in regard to Christians as well. Are Christians usurpers? Have they tried to interpose themselves into this special relationship between God and the Chosen People of Israel? Or have they in some sense used or abused the Jewish tradition, taking it far beyond what imagination could even suggest at times? For example, would the Christian understanding of the covenant and the covenant way be recognizable to a Jew who would have been living at the same time as Saint Paul? I think maybe these are some questions that would be worth pursuing.

L.K.: I would change one word, Peter. I wouldn't say "ambiguity" on the Jewish side towards Christians and Christianity, but rather "distrust." The history of the last 2,000 years hasn't been too kind to us Jews from our point of view. Perhaps we who grew up in the atmosphere of Vatican II and Christian documents on the relationship of Christians and Jews have a different experience from our parents or our grandparents. I speak especially from my own Argentinean-Polish experience. But I think that to continue in distrust is one of the greatest mistakes we are committing today.

One aspect of that distrust is the feeling that the eagerness of Christians to talk to Jews hides the fact that they intend to convert us. And Vatican II was very careful in stressing the lack of any conversionary purpose in the dialogue between Christians and Jews. But I want to point out something, namely, that in dialogue there shouldn't be any proselytizing spirit but the free exercise of the respective faith commitments. Personally, in a dialogue relationship, I want the Christian to be a Christian, and the Jew to be a Jew.

P.S.: Those are the ground rules for any kind of human discussion which seeks to take the dignity of people seriously. So if we can return to Saint Paul, both of us seem to agree that, for better or for worse, he initiated the theological agenda for Jewish-Christian dialogue ever since.

Endnotes
[1] Catholic League for Religious and Civil Rights.
[2] The Anti-Defamation League of B'Nai B'rith.

Chapter Two

Faith, Grace, and Law

Good Works

L.K.: In that spirit, I would like to consider two words. One is "grace," and the other is "law." The Hebrew word for grace is *"Hesed,"* which can be translated as grace, mercy, loving-kindness. *Hesed* is the spirit of God that prompts the Eternal to start a relationship and to establish a covenant. Psalm 136, for example, says, "Give thanks to the Lord, for he is good; his grace *(Hesed)* endures forever." So the idea of *Hesed* relates to manifest acts of God, as for example, creation. In Jewish tradition, God creates the world and the human being for a purpose, for the covenantal relationship that will bring redemption to the world.

Another aspect of *Hesed* relates to two dimensions of Jewish theological thought. One is faith. The other is *"Halakhah"*, called law, although I prefer to use the Hebrew word until we find an English expression that really describes what *Halakhah* is.

The Hebrew word for faith is *"Emunah."* The word is easily recognized by all of us because of the usage of "amen" in our prayers and responses. *Emunah* — faith — is the recognition and the acceptance of God's call and covenant. Faith for Jews is not a "saving" power, if I may use your vocabulary, but a process by which we accept God and make the covenantal relationship a daily, lived reality.

P.S.: As a Catholic, I'm very comfortable with what you have outlined in terms of faith and grace and law. I think you might have more of a challenge if I were a Lutheran. As a matter of fact, one of Luther's biggest contentions against the Catholic Church in the sixteenth century was that he thought we were too Jewish, that our concept of faith was in many ways more of the mentality behind the Epistle of Saint James in the New Testament. James speaks about faith being dead without works, whereas Saint Paul drew the distinction much more sharply between faith and works.

Paul was involved in disputations. And the position that he enunciates in Galatians and then solidifies in Romans is one which needs to be understood and nuanced. For the Catholic Church, there has always been a very carefully worked out interrelationship of faith and works, and not some kind of process external to the individual, but rather an internal response of loving obedience. Therefore, because I am aware of God's *Hesed* — His mercy, His love, His grace, the grace of election — I respond to that call by living a particular kind of life.

L.K.: Many years ago Samuel Sandmel wrote a book called *The Genius of Paul*. There he pointed out the great contribution of Paul to Christianity and also to interreligious dialogue. There is one point that I remember Sandmel stressing in class. It was the fact that in criticizing *Halakhah*, Paul and liberal theological Jews have something in common. They both agree that *Halakhah* emphasizes works rather than spirituality. And now I would agree with him completely, because of my own relationship to *Halakhah*.

Halakhah is for me a way of fulfilling God's commands daily. This fulfilling relates to my present existential experience. That is, I fulfill the *Halakhic* ordinances in a way which is meaningful here and now. That doesn't mean that I have to be selective in what is comfortable for me. This is not what I have in mind. What I mean is that sacredness had a meaning for my grandfather in Poland, and sacredness has another significance for me in a pluralistic society, exposed to Christianity and having close friends who are Christians. This is a unique experience that somewhat enriches my *Halakhic* understanding. *Halakhah* is not an end in itself but a means to make God present in my everyday life.

P.S.: Give me an example of what you're referring to, Leon.

Understanding the Law

L.K.: I will give you an example related also to the New Testament. As you recall, Jesus was criticized because he healed somebody on the *Shabbat* (Sabbath). The text says that the Pharisees criticized him bitterly. The question is that the Pharisaic movement was not monolithic, but was divided into seven groups. When the New Testament was compiled, years after the destruction of the Temple and the dissolution of the Pharisaic movement in general, the text talks about the Pharisees, but it doesn't reflect that there were seven groups within the movement, at times all holding different positions. What Jesus said, that one can transgress the *Shabbat* in order to save a life, is part of the Pharisaic commitment. It is the concept of *pikuah hanefesh*, that is, the saving of a human being goes beyond observances and one can transgress the *Shabbat* in order to save a human being. In that regard I don't mind, for instance, going to a hospital on *Shabbat* because I know a friend needs my prayers. I doubt that God would be offended by such a transgression. I am fulfilling the concept of *pikuah hanefesh* as Jesus did when He saved a life on *Shabbat*.

P.S.: This has always been the Catholic understanding of law as well. You take, for example, our very strong commitment to the Sunday Mass obligation, so strong that in Catholic moral theology to the present day we hold that to miss Mass deliberately on Sunday constitutes a mortal sin, which is to say it breaks one's relationship in a definitive way with Almighty God. Nonetheless, if the law of charity requires that one perform obligations in a home for a sick relative or anything of that nature, then the law is automatically held in abeyance, so that the higher law of love can be fulfilled.

L.K.: Your approach and mine would be the same on this issue; however, it would not be accepted by Orthodoxy, which has a very strict concept about it. I have a more liberal — if I may use that word — approach to *Halakhah*.

But please do not misunderstand. For me, this *Halakhah* is crucial in the daily performance of my religiosity. I translate my religious life by certain physical or public representations. For example, I think of having my head covered. Jews in southern France in the Middle Ages were not covered when they went into the streets. But for me, out of my own experience, to wear my *yarmulke* is a way of expressing my daily recognition of God's presence and of professing it to the world. I would say that act is part of my faith, a faithfulness to living in the loving presence of God.

26

P.S.: In some conversations with fundamentalist Christians, I have had to try to explain a little better this relationship of faith and works in the Catholic scheme of things. An explanation that I have found helpful is that one is certainly saved by faith in Jesus Christ, from the Christian perspective, but it's not an automatic process. Therefore, works are involved, but one is not saved *by* works, but *to* works.

Once again, this is the response to the realization that one is called, redeemed, saved, however you choose to phrase it. This is the very important human dimension. At times in some brands of Christianity, the sovereignty of God is so stressed, which is obviously important, but the concomitant difficulty is that the human response and human dignity are not taken seriously enough. As a result, one can almost say that we're saved in spite of ourselves, whether we want to be saved or not, whether we want to have a relationship or not. And in effect this makes God violate human respect, dignity, and free will, in order to save us whether or not we want it.

Authority and Interpretation

L.K.: We have been talking about grace and *Halakhah*, and there is one additional matter that requires our attention. That is the question of religious authority. I feel uneasy that I can choose *Halakhically*, and that I have no supreme authority to tell me what to do or not to do. I am challenged by *Halakhah* to lead a very creative, religious Jewish life. But I also realize that I can use *Halakhah* to the point of absurdity. This is quite a danger, and our community is aware of that. We don't have a central authority, as does the Catholic Church, a magisterium, but our consensus comes from the acceptance by the community, mainly through rabbinic leadership, which plays a pivotal role in our life in matters related to religious observance.

P.S.: In Catholicism, we view the magisterium of the Church in many ways simply as an extension of the principle of the Incarnation. Historically, Christianity is comfortable with the whole question of human mediation. Now at this point we have to lay aside various forms of Protestantism which are rather skittish in regard to human mediation. But certainly Roman Catholicism and Eastern Orthodoxy would find this as a natural conclusion of an incarnational religion.

Let me ask you, Leon, what role there is for a formal or standardized interpretation of particular texts, whether those are biblical or non-biblical, in various branches of Judaism.

L.K.: Interpretation is basic in the Jewish approach to the Hebrew Bible. We have commentaries from practically the very beginning of the compilation of the Bible. The *Mishnah*, for example, is a *Halakhic* commentary on the Bible: that is, how to implement God's commandments in everyday life. There is also an existential interpretation in the *Midrash*, a methodology very well known by Jesus and expressed in many New Testament texts. Most interpretation was given by the Talmud, both the Jerusalem version and the Babylonian version.

Explanation is key, especially in our days. After Auschwitz we need to interpret God's Word in view of the Kingdom of Evil. Interpretation has allowed us to make the biblical Word come alive through the centuries. And in this respect, I want to repeat some words of a very important thinker in Judaism who wrote a long study on interpretation. Simon Rawidowicz says the following that requires our understanding and reflection:

"In contradistinction to *explicatio* and *commentatio*, I would understand by *interpretatio*, with which I deal here, an attempt at reshaping either the 'document' interpreted or the world it came from. Here an act of transference is always involved. An invasion of one system by another takes place. *Interpretatio* lives by crisis in various degrees. The crisis that stimulates it will become its criterion. *Interpretatio* can be characterized by a particular attitude of the *interpreter* who struggles between preserving and rejecting some forms or content of the world at his interpretive 'mercy,' by a tension between continuation and rebellion, tradition, and innovation."

These words describe what interpretation has meant, and means today, in our living experience of the Word of God.

P.S.: My question, I guess, would be: How would a Jew react to, let's say, the statement of the Second Vatican Council, that for Catholics we have, in a sense, three realities that we're concerned with in perceiving or accepting divine revelation? The written Word of God, the community which receives and transmits that Word, and then the authority which interprets it: those would be the three pillars of biblical interpretation for Catholics. As you are well aware, with fundamentalist Christians, for example, it's the Word and only the Word, and it's a disembodied Word, at least from the Catholic perspective.

L.K.: For us interpretation is to bring new dimensions of the biblical Word. That is, that the revelation of God is not complete, but it's open to an amplification of

29

the meaning related to specific experiences. This does not mean to make it easier or more difficult, but to make it meaningful. Interpretation is essentially that, to make meaningful the Word of God. At this time in our history, after what happened in Europe, in the Holocaust, we need an interpretation and reinterpretation of the Word of God for our everyday life. Sometimes I say that what we need is a new *Halakhah*, a new way, a new manner of implementing God's voice in the midst of the Kingdom of Evil and after it.

Amplification of Meaning

P.S.: When I heard you use the word "amplification," immediately came to mind a very important and basic principle in Catholic exegesis, which is called the *sensus plenior*. We see it as God giving us the opportunity actually to see more in a text today than perhaps the original inspired writer was aware of. This is a classic way of interpreting the Hebrew Scriptures for Christians, namely, that there is more than meets the eye. For example, the Isaiah passage in reference to Hezekiah's heir. Christians see in that text a prophecy of the Virgin Birth of Jesus. In all likelihood, First Isaiah never had such a concept in mind. But because of the build-up of the experience of living with the reality of that Word and living as God's community, we can see things there that perhaps were not visible to the naked eye to begin with.

L.K.: Your reference to Isaiah and a Christian interpretation hits on a delicate matter. That is the question of the use and abuse of the biblical text for purposes that are not related to the text itself. I would say that the way the Church Fathers approached the Hebrew Bible was to find indications of the coming of Jesus. In that way, passages like Jeremiah 31 about a new covenant are taken as a reference or a hint about the coming of Jesus and the covenant with Christianity. This requires a very careful joint approach.

P.S.: I empathize with Jewish concerns in this regard. However, from the Patristic period or the Age of the Fathers of the Church, it has always been the Christian position that the Old Testament, or the Hebrew Scriptures, are enlightened by the New and the New is clarified by the Old. So there's a kind of ebb and flow or a constant interchange between the two covenants. I don't think it needs to be seen in a negative light. Again, I can appreciate the concern that it could be seen as *only* a preparation. On the other hand, if God is involved in an ongoing process of the revelation of Himself to the human race, to humanity in general, to Abraham and the Chosen People, and to the Church, this need not be seen in any way as a negative assessment of the relationship between God and the Jews, or as using a text in an improper manner. Furthermore, it is important to note that the Fathers, and even the New Testament authors, saw the Hebrew Scriptures as very much their own possession, not something that was borrowed but something that was theirs by right.

L.K.: Our discussion should take us to a consideration of the first century. You recall that Saint Paul spoke of Christianity as a shoot "grafted" onto Judaism. I have the idea, and have written about it on several occasions, that we should use Paul's image but apply it to both Judaism and Christianity. That means that in the first century two branches were grafted into the tree of the Hebrew Bible.

One was the rabbinic explanation from the Pharisaic movement that created rabbinic theology, and the other was the branch of Jesus toward the world. Naturally, this is not an idea that can be accepted by my Orthodox brothers and sisters, but the more I think about that period, the more I'm inclined to call it First Century. It was the first century for us, because we went from biblical Jewish experience to rabbinic Judaism by the expounding of the meaning of the Hebrew Bible for that period. And also, there is the appearance of Jesus and his vocation to the world.

Belief in the Afterlife

P.S.: You know, Leon, we've been talking about the whole question of *Halakhah* and how one develops a relationship with God or how God develops a relationship with an individual, and certainly one of the overriding concerns in Christianity is the whole question of an afterlife. I'm well aware of the fact that at the time of Jesus this was a very controversial point, but perhaps our readers would be interested in knowing some of the history of the Jewish understanding of the afterlife.

When I used to teach high school, I can remember saying to the students when teaching them the Ten Commandments, "Now believe it or not, when Moses gave these commandments to his people, they were not people who were going to live by these commandments because of a fear of punishment in an afterlife or a hope of a reward in an afterlife." So there was a whole different psychology and theology and philosophy of obedience to the law. And I think some Christians are surprised to discover that everything need not hang on an afterlife, although for us Christians it is an absolute, but for a different reason. I'd be interested in some analysis of the question from a contemporary Jewish perspective.

L.K.: If you would ask a Jewish person with no theological background, but a person who lives every day and works hard for his family, whether he or she believes in the afterlife, that person might respond merely, "No." Afterlife is not a central concept in Jewish life. What is important for us is life, this life given by God, this world in which we live, and for that reason, when we toast, we say "*l'chaim*," that is, "to life," for the goodness and beauty of life.

I would say that the concept of afterlife has gone through a whole development from biblical times to our days. In biblical days it appears as a sort of rest, with the soul resting after all the struggles in life. For example, in Samuel we have that anecdote where Saul asks the soul of Samuel to come back and Samuel complains of the fact that he was awakened from a restful dream. I would say that the concept of afterlife has been very much influenced by Christianity. This is ironic, because we believe that Christianity owes everything to Judaism, while we are uneasy to believe that Judaism has taken ideas from Christianity. When I was in the seminary, I took a whole course in Christian influences on Judaism, and I recently wrote an article on that subject. There are ideas and concepts resulting from Christian influences. For example, there is a period in the Middle Ages where devotion to the dead was central. Judaism responded by developing its own ideas about afterlife, but it's related to those historical circumstances. What is important also is that we in our liturgy don't have a specific prayer for the dead. We use the *Kaddish*. But if you read the *Kaddish* prayer in the original, it has no reference at all to death. It is a collection of nouns and adjectives praising the majesty and glory of God; it has become, however, a sort of sacrosanct expression of a liturgy related to the dead. Even Jews who are not committed religiously will make a point to go once a year to the synagogue to say *Kaddish* in memory of a deceased father or mother or other relative. But *Kaddish* developed at the time of the great fashion of the Mass for the Dead and the cult of the afterlife. I would say essentially that the emphasis for us is life rather than afterlife.

Resurrection of the Dead

P.S.: May I bring you back just a bit more to the whole question of the development of the concept of the resurrection of the dead, in Judaism and in that intertestamental period, and specifically as Christians would be familiar with the confrontation which Paul instigated between the Pharisees and the Sadducees in his own trial?

L.K.: We believe in resurrection, though many Jews won't accept that concept. That is ironic. In one of our prayers, we thank God for the fact that He brings the dead to life. So this prayer, which is part of our morning and evening services, reflects the idea that there is a resurrection when the Kingdom of God comes to earth, and that people will come back to life, rather than in a special part of the world that can be called Paradise or Hell. Is that clear?

P.S.: Yes. I would ask further, what would be the responses today in the various branches of Judaism, to the question of afterlife, reward, punishment, things of that nature?

L.K.: There's no easy answer. You do realize, Peter, after so many years in contact with Jews, that there are no easy responses in Judaism. I wouldn't say that all Orthodox believe in resurrection. Some people might feel that when the Messiah comes, everybody will come back. In the Conservative movement, there are some people who believe in resurrection and others who do not. In the Reform movement, I would say that in general few believe in resurrection.

Hierarchy and Community

P.S.: There is one matter that we have yet to consider. That is the question of hierarchy and community structure.

L.K.: In the Jewish community, when we think about hierarchy, we immediately think of the Catholic Church rather than our own community. In our community there is no hierarchy because we don't have a central authority like the Pope, though we have federations of rabbis, like the Central Conference of American Rabbis or the Rabbinical Assembly. But they don't have the sort of magisterium of the Catholic Church that implies the authority of the Pope and the bishops together. There is, in effect, a magisterium in Jewish life, and that is the consensus of the community-at-large or groups of the community concerning certain matters related to religious life. A new *Halakhic* position will be accepted by the community-at-large or by a body of rabbis, but there is no central authority that says the last word. Even the chief rabbis in Israel, both the Sephardic and the Ashkenazi, do not have an authority similar to the Pope in the Catholic Church. It is an *Halakhic* opinion, but not the last word, concerning customs or religious observances.

P.S.: You mentioned, Leon, that when Jews hear the word "hierarchy," they immediately think of the Catholic Church. That's rather interesting, because I think most Catholics would say that we are a hierarchical Church because of our roots in Judaism. What would have caused that change? The destruction of the Temple and the priesthood, I guess, would have been seriously influential in that regard, but anything else?

L.K.: I would say the historical experience in the West. The Jewish community could not exercise, up to the nineteenth century, total freedom of religion. They were under the control of the landed aristocracy or under Christian ecclesiastical control, and for that reason we did not develop a centralized hierarchy. The Catholic Church might have learned about religious authority from reading the Hebrew Bible or rabbinic writings, but that was twenty centuries ago when that kind of hierarchy existed. After Constantine, we lost that form of ecclesiastical structure and located authority in rabbis, rabbinical schools, or communities.

P.S.: In Catholicism, we use a theological aphorism: *Lex orandi, lex credendi* (the law of believing is the law of praying). In other words, you can discover what we believe from the prayers we say. In that connection, as we now prepare to discuss prayer in our respective traditions, are there any additional matters that should be addressed as a foundation before we approach God in prayer — or *as* we approach Him?

Prayer and Suffering

L.K.: The question of prayer and liturgy is central in

the present discussion of the meaning and future of spirituality in Judaism. Especially after the impact of the Holocaust, there is a serious concern among many congregants about how to direct your prayers and to whom you direct your prayers. The old way, the way of pure transcendental language, is not appealing for many, many people in our community. I remember congregants coming to me and asking a very simple question: "How can we talk about the omnipotence of God after Auschwitz?" And this is a question that related not only to my congregants, but also to me personally. Every time I visit the site of a former concentration camp, I am confronted with the question of, "Where was God?" because if God is so powerful as described in my prayers, why didn't He confront the murderers?

So, in liturgy and prayer, our main concern nowadays is towards an understanding of God, His essence and being at the end of the twentieth century.

P.S.: It's interesting that you would talk about the difficulty of prayer in the face of suffering and disaster because, ironically, today as we get together for this section, the Catholic Church celebrates the Feast of the Triumph of the Cross. The purpose of the feast is to celebrate with greater solemnity what we Christians celebrate on Good Friday. So often this is difficult for people outside the Faith to understand, that we can actually celebrate an apparently ignominious, ignoble defeat and total destruction of a Person. For us Christians, and particularly those in the Catholic way of life, we see suffering as a purifying experience and, amazingly enough perhaps, demonstrating the very depths of both divine love and divine omnipotence. Thus, it's not a negative for us. As a matter of fact, I prayed this morning in our general intercessions for the sick and suffering, who could begin to understand their suffering through the Jesus Who suffered and triumphed over and through that suffering. It is, obviously, a very different approach and experience, but for us suffering does not connote the same as it does for the Jewish community.

L.K.: The Hebrew word for prayer is *tefilah*, and its root denotes a dimension of judgment. So the Hebrew word for prayer entails judgment, and perhaps this is our approach to the concept of God. We are looking at God and judging God, which is an old idea of Judaism, to be in a constant state of discussion and sometimes verbal fighting, as you can see in the Book of Job and other books of the Bible. Now many of our theologians are judging God for His supposed absence at Auschwitz.

The question of suffering is different in our understanding. I feel, personally, that I cannot accept a concept of God in which God might be indifferent to the death of children. I know it personally, very personally, and also in the case of the Second World War, when many of my cousins who were children were thrown into the gas chambers. Is that pleasing to God, as He would appear in certain strata of biblical thought? Perhaps it had meaning 2,500 years ago, but it is very difficult for me to accept it today. I feel that the understanding of God and religiosity go through a process of deepening their meaning, deepening their understanding of God, and projecting them into the contemporary scene. Otherwise, one lives constantly in a sort of antiquated understanding of God and the relationship with God.

P.S.: I do not view, and I don't think Catholic theology views, suffering as pleasing to God at an objective level. For us, the God Who permits suffering was not absent from suffering in the death of His Son, nor is He absent from suffering in the death or suffering of any other innocent beings. This is an aspect of Christian theology which is very important to understand. While we certainly would hold to the Jewish notion of the absolute transcendence of God, we also hold very strongly, because of the Incarnation of Christ, to the immanence of God, that God is very close to His people. Of course, that's not absent from Jewish theology either. Certainly in the Old Testament when the Chosen People suffered, it is clear that God was present in that suffering. He identifies with the suffering of His people. I think it's raised to a different level, a stronger level, in Christianity because of the sufferings of Christ.

Cleansing of Words?

L.K.: Perhaps what we need, Peter, is a sort of a cleansing of words. For example, let us call the Hebrew Bible "Hebrew Bible" or *Tanach*, rather than "Old Testament." We feel in the Jewish community that the term "Old Testament" projects a negative approach to the biblical experience of the Jewish people. This has been a question of confrontation for centuries and should be overcome in our present conversation.

P.S.: I have no problem in referring to what Christians see as the Old Testament as the Hebrew Scriptures. That's no problem for us whatsoever, but I would also like to make it very clear that when the Church speaks of the Old Testament, and surely when I speak of the Old Testament, that in no way is to be perceived as a negative comment. For me, in particular, "old" does not imply antiquated or useless. It implies the first, and sometimes things that are older are actually better. "Old" unfortunately, perhaps, has come to mean displaced or put to one side, but that's a more modern problem than it is a uniquely Catholic problem.

L.K.: Perhaps we should go back to our consideration of the concept of suffering in Judaism and Christianity.

P.S.: Leon, you used a verb in talking about human suffering and God, that you could not appreciate a God Who would be pleased with the death or the suffering of innocents. I think there are certain brands of Christianity, surely large groups of fundamentalist Christians, and perhaps certain forms of Catholic spirituality, which looked on even the death of Christ as necessary to please an almost bloodthirsty God. These are aberrant strains in Christianity. In the purest forms of Christian theology we never, never talk about God needing to be appeased by someone's blood or someone's life or anything of that nature. So I think once that is clear, you and I are probably much closer on the whole question of suffering. Suffering for a Christian is something that is evil, something to be avoided at all costs. If we look at the life and ministry of Jesus, we see that when He came across sin, suffering, disease, even death, the whole purpose of His ministry was to counteract those things, because they are negative in terms of the coming Kingdom of God. Those things, then, are not to be perceived as positive. I think the difference comes when the suffering is indeed inevitable, when I have done everything possible to avoid the suffering and it is still real, I am still going to die, I will still perhaps contract a terminal disease, or someone who is near and dear to me has this problem; at that moment I simply say, I cannot plumb any further the mystery of God's Providence and I accept what's given, and then as a Christian, I am united to the sufferings and death of Christ.

Suffering and Death

L.K.: Suffering has a different significance in Judaism. In a first meaning in biblical days, suffering was seen as the result of transgressing God's law and God's resultant punishment. This line continued through the centuries, though in the rabbinic days in the first centuries of the Common Era, the response was different. There was the idea that suffering is part of the human situation, and part of the human experience. And that's what I think personally. Suffering is part of my condition, and this relates very closely to a personal family experience. We lost one of our daughters, Myriam Gabriela, in a car accident. For — I would say for years — I struggled with the meaning of what happened. I was unconscious for two weeks after the accident, so I cannot remember exactly what happened, but there was a sense of guilt, that is, that I was driving the car and I produced the accident, though legally no one could determine how the accident occurred. This was a mystery of life that transcended, for me, my experience of such an event.

I asked myself for many years what was the meaning of Myriam's death. Did it have any significance? I was very doubtful, and I do remember going to the cemetery to pray for her and to scream at God: Why did He allow such a thing? And after a while I realized that it was beyond God's dominion to stop a car or to stop history or to save lives. I think that God has given me an obligation, and that obligation is to be responsible for life. I don't believe that the accident was destiny, God's design, or a punishment for my sins, because I asked myself how much did I sin that I deserved the death of a child? I should be punished with my death if death is a punishment, rather than the death of a child. Myriam's death relates to a human situation. Was I driving wrongly, or was the other driver driving wrongly? I really don't know.

P.S.: You mentioned a couple of things which resonate well with the Catholic approach to death. First of all, that death is a normal part of human existence. It's a part of our nature as finite beings. Sometimes in Christian theology we prognosticate on what life would have been had Adam not sinned. And there are some schools of thought which suggest that if Adam hadn't sinned, suffering would not have entered the world, work would not have been necessary for man, and most importantly, man would never have died. I don't tend to subscribe to that school of thought. I think labor and suffering and death are constant and probably necessary reminders to man that we are finite beings, and therefore not excused from the lot of finitude. Therefore, these things are important for us to understand, as you say, as part of an overall plan of human existence. Saint Thomas Aquinas is very careful to note in his *Summa,*[1] for example, that while God could in His complete omnipotence intervene at every moment of human existence, in fact He has set up a certain plan or order of creation which plays itself out, except for the most extraordinary reasons (for instance, the Exodus of the Hebrews from Egypt). Whether or not God personally intervened with each and every one of those plagues, whether God personally parted the waters of the sea, those are questions that I guess exegetes can play with from now until the end of time. But certainly those are extraordinary events in order to advance God's plan of salvation. But in the normal course of events, if you and I walk across First Avenue this afternoon and carelessly step out in front of a car and get hit, it would be presumptuous for us to expect God to lift the car from our path so that we can continue to walk through. Or if a man is driving drunk and hits us, we can hardly expect God to intervene at that moment and to say, "There's a nice rabbi and a nice priest there. Let's not hit them, and let's let him hit something else."

L.K.: What you say relates very well to my own personal experience. I have been asked many times how I react to the deaths in the concentration camps or to the death of my daughter. And my response has always been very clear. I think of Myriam looking at me, being at my side, and being a little bit upset with my constant mourning. I felt that Myriam was telling me, "Go ahead. You have an obligation for the rest of society, for the other two children, for wife and family and friends, for the community-at-large." That suffering shouldn't be an end in itself, only a way or at times a moment in life. The most important thing is life itself, our obligation to it, our creativity and expounding its human possibilities.

P.S.: I've never had to deal with the problem of a tragic death at a very personal level. The deaths of my grandparents and the death of my father were very much in the normal course of events. Two pastoral situations, however, have touched and moved me very deeply. My first funeral as a priest was for a boy who was a student in the high school where I was an administrator. He and another boy had been drinking too much. The two of them were in a car. The boy who was the driver was killed instantaneously. The other boy was barely injured, and this boy, interestingly enough, had always been interested in the priesthood and had wavered considerably in his junior and senior years of high school, then had gotten involved with some problems — certainly with alcohol or perhaps with drugs — and the first thing that this boy said to me at the wake service of his dear, dear friend of twelve years was, "Father, my buddy has died so that I could come to my senses and live properly again." That was a tremendous insight for a 17-year-old boy.

The second pastoral situation was a Funeral Mass that I had to celebrate the day after Christmas for a family who had lost a four-year-old child to leukemia. I racked my brain and prayed for the whole three days, wondering what I would ever say of any significance, any meaning, to these poor people. As you know, the death of a child is so horrible, but of all times for us — for the child to die the day before Christmas, and here we were to bury her the day after Christmas. I searched my brain and heart and all I could come up with was to say, "Christmas celebrates the gift of God's Son to the human race. God loved you enough to give you this child. Now do you love God enough to give your child back to God as your Christmas gift to Him?" Now, to someone who is outside the notions of faith and relationships with the Divine, it's impossible to understand. It's a cruel God, and we as clergy are simply trying to put Band-Aids on wounds which can't be healed. In point of fact, those people fifteen years later still tell me that every year on Christmas, in a sense, they reoffer the gift of their daughter to God.

L.K.: Let me finish this part of our conversation with one phrase: Let us say yes to life. Yes to life, despite memories of the past, the pain of the people we loved who are gone but present in our everyday life, and the horrors of history. Yes to life, in the sense of continuing, despite life itself, our obligation to creation and to God's commandment to re-create creation.

Endnotes
[1]The *Summa Theologiae* of Saint Thomas is a major work of Catholic theology.

Chapter Three

Communion With God

The Work of the People

P.S.: When we talk about liturgy, we know that it comes from Greek words that mean "the work of the people," in the sense of the community, the assembly of the faithful, whose first obligation in life is to worship Almighty God. One of the problems we have had in the Catholic community in the past twenty-five years in the wake of the Second Vatican Council is that sometimes we've been so concerned about altering or modifying the liturgical forms that we have forgotten, at least in this country, that our primary purpose in liturgy is the worship of God and not the worship of man. And so there's a transcendent element that has to be emphasized here.

Leon, how has the Jewish community dealt with this phenomenon?

L.K.: I cannot separate the life of my family or my people from prayer. When I go to the synagogue in the morning or Friday night for a *Shabbat* service, I need a few minutes of inner silence. It's a silence that allows me to be cleansed from work, from the problems of everyday life in a big city, to relate to the people I love, and finally to God. Those are the stages. Then, at the end of my silence, I feel that I'm in communion with God. I use the word "communion" though it's not totally part of our Jewish tradition. There are words in the Hebrew vocabulary that can be translated as "communion." But I feel that it is essential in the process of prayer to start in silence, to search for God, to be in communion with God, and then to go into the structure of prayer.

P.S.: This notion of communion with God is obviously central to the religious experience of all people, but certainly to both the Jewish and Catholic approach to liturgy. Sometimes people get the impression that all we Catholics do is a lot of formalized mumbo-jumbo, and they would say the Jews are not far behind in the game. But I think that's to misunderstand. If that is the impression that you or I or our people have created, then that's unfortunate. If that's an impression that is held by people who do not really know who we are and what we do, then it's part of our responsibility to correct that impression.

For us Catholics, private prayer and liturgical prayer go hand in hand. They are inseparable from each other. If all a Catholic does is worship God for forty-five minutes at Sunday Mass, in all likelihood he has a rather inadequate life of worship. It's not surprising, for example, that young people will say, "I get nothing out of Mass." The standard line in reply is, "What did you put into it?" But equally, "Is this the only time during the week that you are trying to pray?" No surprise, then, if that's the case, that one finds liturgical prayer very difficult. The individual human person cannot "turn on" to God in a forty-five-minute period. Nor can one be expected to be sensitive to the movings or the promptings of Almighty God in a very short period of time. The example I always give to young people is married life. The peak moment of communication between a husband and wife is obviously the time of sexual intercourse. It's not called intercourse by accident;

that's because it's a moment of great interpersonal communication. But if the only time a couple try to communicate with each other is for the five or ten minutes of sexual relations, whether that's every day or once a week or once a month or once a year, there's no surprise that it is ultimately a rather dissatisfying experience.

So there needs to be a total communication between the creature and the Creator on a regular, ongoing basis. For us Catholics, that comes through individual, personal, private prayer, through the reading of the Scriptures, perhaps through the recitation of the Rosary, through personal meditation, through spiritual reading; some people even go to daily Mass or recite the Liturgy of the Hours, which we'll talk about in a little bit, and then finally, the peak moment, yes, the Sunday Eucharist.

Types of Judaism

L.K.: Communication is the key word. It is central in the daily liturgy of the Jewish people. In our morning service, for example, there are two distinct areas. One is private prayer, which you do before going to the synagogue, and then the prayer of the synagogue when we need ten men present at the service if it's an Orthodox congregation, or ten men or women if it's a Conservative or Reform congregation.

At this point, it's important to explain the differences between Conservative, Orthodox, and Reform Judaism. Orthodoxy is the classical interpretation of the biblical experience of Israel. It has grown out of the rabbinic explanation of the biblical text of the first century, translated in the *Mishnah* and *Midrash*, and later on in the medieval commentaries, up to contemporary theological understandings of God and Israel. The *Mishnah* is the "legal" or religious interpretation of the biblical text. The *Mishnah*, for example, has a section on the celebration of the *Shabbat*, how to light the candles, when to light the candles, how long is the *Shabbat* rest, etc.; that is, the *Mishnah* explains in detail what was indicated in the biblical text. Books of the Talmud, both the Jerusalem and the Babylonian Talmudim, are commentaries of the *Mishnah* and the *Midrash*. The latter is the literary interpretation of the Bible. As you know, it has influenced very deeply the writing of the New Testament. The infancy stories of Jesus are based on the *Midrashic* texts.

The Conservative and Reform movements are new attempts to live the covenantal relationship God-Israel. This is not a new phenomenon in Jewish life. Tradition and change are the inner dimensions of our constant effort — I should say eternal effort — to understand God's call and our mission to witness the covenant.

P.S.: What are the main concepts of both movements?

L.K.: Reform Judaism started in Germany in the nineteenth century. The main difference with Orthodoxy was, and still is, the authority of *Halakhah*. Orthodoxy affirms the divine authority of *Halakhah*, while Reform Judaism subjects *Halakhah*, or religious law, to the judgment and life experience of the community.

The movement was and is interested in liturgy, meaningful and creative, including music following the psalm tradition, incorporating women actively in the liturgies, sharing spirit and space with men, though in Orthodox synagogues women are separated and do not count for the *minyan*, or minimum of ten men for prayers.

Reform has changed and is changing theologically. Presently, there is a tendency to incorporate traditional thinking and customs into the liturgy and sacred calendar. Tradition becomes a way, not an end by itself. The Reform movement in the U.S.A. has anointed women as rabbis, a trend that is now followed by the Conservative movement.

P.S.: What are the ideas of the Conservative movement?

L.K.: The Conservative movement is a religious current that originated in the U.S.A. but is rooted in Europe, especially the nineteenth century, to bring religious life to modern times without sacrificing tradition. *Halakhah* should be adapted to present life in a creative manner. Though I studied at a Reform seminary, I personally feel very comfortable with this idea as reflected in daily spirituality and prayer. Abraham J. Heschel was the great theologian of the movement, and his influence is still felt among Conservative and Reform Jews.

The contribution of Conservative and Reform Judaism is a new appreciation of tradition, of the implementation of *Halakhah*, and meaningful prayer in the reality of our time.

P.S.: Given the differences among the three groups of Jewish tradition, what might you identify as common elements in the daily synagogue service?

L.K.: I would say that the main concepts of prayer in the three denominations are God, the unity and uniqueness of God, Israel as a community, and Torah and study. That is, that we worship one God, we do it together as the

People of Israel, and we are obligated to study the Torah every day, and especially during the weekly reading on Saturday morning.

Though the three groups share the basic ideas, they are expressed in different ways in the prayer book. The Orthodox prayer book is very long — I would say too long, because I pray at an Orthodox synagogue every day — and has incorporated not only the prayers of 2,000 years ago, but added materials of the Middle Ages and prayers of our own days. So in an Orthodox service, the rabbi or the cantor will not read the whole prayer book, but will chant only certain sections, or will chant the first verse of the page and the last verse. This irritates me very much. For me, prayer is the way to be in communion with God. Even if I don't accept the meaning of that prayer, it makes me feel close to God. And if the prayer is mumbled, then I don't feel that is any way to reach God; it is only that — mumbling.

P.S.: This is, of course, one of the things that fundamentalist Christians would identify about Catholicism to which they would object; namely, they would see a kind of empty formalism or ritualism that is content with repeating the form with no substance beneath it. I think that's an unfair criticism of us today. It could have happened, let's say, thirty years ago in some of our earlier liturgical forms where it was not supposed to be done, but an individual priest may have done it (and precisely what you say, recite the first line, mumble through the middle, and give an outloud ending to it). I think that we must, both of us, as liturgical bodies, as liturgical communities, guard against that kind of formalism, which really can be scandalous to people outside, and sometimes causes anger to us who really do believe, because we see this as a prostitution of liturgical worship.

L.K.: What you said has been reflected in the liturgical experiences of the Conservative and Reform movements. Both of them have created, based on the classical text of the *Siddur* (the prayer book), texts that reflect our present experience in the world and our experience with God. Both liturgies keep the original Hebrew text, but the translations are meaningful translations that relate to our situation. And here I want to clarify a matter. I want a prayer that is meaningful to me at this time of my life in history, but I don't want something so contemporary that one month from now it might sound out of place. This I cannot accept. What I want is a prayer that reflects my search for God, a prayer for a human being who lives at the end of the twentieth century, in the midst of a noisy civilization like our American experience, in a society where values are deteriorating and the family is in danger of disintegrating because of many problems. There is also the fact that our community is not the same community known by my parents fifty or sixty years ago. History has changed, and it has to be reflected in our communion with God. And this should be the great challenge of liturgy, not to be a fashionable prayer, but a contemporary prayer related to my human situation, an eternal situation, vis-à-vis God.

P.S.: Leon, you touch on several issues that have been quite neuralgic with the Catholic community of the United States for the past thirty years. Of all the Jews I know, you've certainly gone to many Masses, perhaps more than some Catholics. And so you know some of the difficulties that we have faced liturgically in our efforts at reform in the past three decades. I have gone on public record noting that I think many of our efforts have been less than happy. You talk about language, you talk about the content of prayer; these are important issues for us Catholics as well. When we went from an exclusively or almost exclusively sacral language liturgy, for us Latin, to a vernacular, we encountered many, many difficulties. I am not at all opposed to a vernacular liturgy. I see a great deal of benefit in many ways to that. I'm distressed that we in some sense have thrown out the baby with the bath water. In most of our parishes, we have gotten rid of all Latin, and I think the Latin helped do a number of things. First of all, it grounded us in tradition. It reminded us that we Catholics in America belong to a universal Church. It enabled us to be hospitable and welcoming of Catholics from anywhere in the world. And, perhaps most importantly, it kept us from becoming trendy in our notions of theology and in the language that we bring to prayer. I've been very involved in liturgical translation work over the years, and the pitfalls that you describe are common, I think, to anyone who had a sacral language, from which he tries to move to a vernacular. It's got to be faithful to the original text. At the same time, it has to use language which people today can understand and to which they can relate. And yet it can come off like either the sports or comic page of the daily newspaper.

L.K.: We have problems in common, but I'm sure we also have in common certain liturgical customs and liturgical practices. I know that in the Catholic Church you use a lectionary. What is essential in a lectionary?

P.S.: Well, as you know very well, our idea of a lectionary comes from the Jewish idea of a schedule of Bible reading. *"Lectio"* in Latin means "a reading." And prior to the Second Vatican Council, the Catholic Church had a one-year cycle of Scripture readings. For the most part, on Sundays, Catholics were exposed to one of the Epistles of the New Testament and the Gospel passage. On rarer occasions, the congregation was exposed to the Prophets or the historical books of the Hebrew Scriptures. In the revised lectionary, since the 1970s, the Sunday liturgy operates on a three-year cycle of readings. The first reading is generally a passage from the Hebrew Scriptures, and it's designed to dovetail with the Gospel passage of the day. Thus, if something is discussed in one of the four Gospels, there is an attempt to find a passage from the Hebrew Bible which parallels it in some way. For example, the Sunday in which Jesus cures the lepers, the passage for the First Reading might be the Scripture of Naaman the Syrian being healed of his leprosy. The First Reading is followed by a psalm, which is preferably sung, or else recited. That is followed by a Second Reading which is always a New Testament passage from either the Acts of the Apostles or one of the Epistles, and then, finally, the Gospel passage, depending on the year, A, B, or C; A is generally from Matthew, B from Mark, and C from Luke, with John scattered among the three years. That is the format of the Sunday lectionary. The weekday lectionary is a two-year cycle, with the First Reading being either Hebrew Scriptures or Epistles, and those alternate from year one and two, and then the Gospel passage.

L.K.: In the synagogue, we read the Bible on Thursdays and Saturdays in the morning service. The readings are for one year, though some congregations still have the whole reading of the first five books of the Bible in a period of three years. The reading on Saturday morning was followed, centuries ago, by discussions on the meaning of the text. That was the beginning of the *Midrashic* literature — that is, commentaries on the Bible. As you recall from the New Testament, Jesus discusses the biblical text when He goes to the synagogue. That was a typical experience in the first century.

The reading of the Torah is accompanied by a reading from the Prophets. I confess that the Torah portion is too long. Sometimes it's three or more chapters. They are read in toto in many communities, especially in Orthodox communities. Sometimes I see people talking to one other at that moment, communicating thoughts that do not necessarily belong to the reading of the Torah but often relate to family or business problems. And I can understand — that's a natural reaction. When I had a congregation in Argentina, on Saturday morning the cantor or I would not read the whole Torah portion. We would read a certain section, followed by an explanation and a discussion with the community. In that way the Word of God became central in the worship of Saturday morning and allowed the congregants to have a sense of liveliness, of passion for the biblical text and its explanation. I suggested the same ritual in one of the congregations that I attend now, and I was nearly thrown out for being a pagan, which I'm not. But I do feel, as it was 2,000 years ago, that the text has to be central in the liturgical experience of the community. Otherwise, it is just the recitation of a text.

P.S.: For the benefit of our Jewish readers, who may not be familiar with the structure of Catholic worship, the biblical section of our worship service is referred to as the Liturgy of the Word, and unlike the classical Jewish approach, we have very bite-size portions of Scripture. So, if you put our three Scripture passages together and read them non-stop, it wouldn't take ten minutes. At Sunday Mass, it is required that the priest preach a homily or sermon which arises from the biblical text and applies that text to the lives of the people. At weekday Mass, a homily is not required, but is strongly encouraged and certainly so during Advent and Lent, which are two very special times of preparation in the Christian calendar.

Homilies and Hatred

L.K.: The priestly homily is of great concern for me as one involved with the Jewish-Christian dialogue. Homilies through the centuries have been sources of anti-Semitism or hatred toward Jewish neighbors or the Jewish community.

You said previously that the Hebrew Bible portion dovetails with the reading of the New Testament. My thought is: Is it a text used as a pretext for something else? That is, is the text of the Hebrew Bible used to stress the promise of Jesus, or that Jesus crowns Abraham's Covenant? Recently, I have discussed this matter with the National Conference of Catholic Bishops-Secretariat of Catholic-Jewish Relations and the Liturgical Press. The Liturgical Press is very sensitive to this matter and has asked for the preparation of a set of short commentaries, one minute or a minute-and-a-half, for those texts of the New Testament that refer to Jews and Judaism. Those explanations are not intended to change the text of the New Testament, which is sacred. What we need is an explanation, in order to avoid anti-Semitism or hatred against the Jewish people.

P.S.: You raise two related but distinct issues in regard to Christian preaching and use of the Hebrew Scriptures. The first would be, I guess, what in Christianity we've called for a long time the prefigurement of the New in the Old. For us, this goes back 2,000 years; it's found even in the preaching of the apostles, namely, that the Hebrew Scriptures prepare people for the coming of Jesus as Messiah and Lord. I would be less than honest if I said that we do not think that's the case. All of the Fathers of the Church use that form of exegesis of the Hebrew Scriptures. And this approach is so rooted in Christian theology as to be impossible even if it were desirable to change at this point. This should not be done in a way that suggests that Judaism is incomplete or, much less, that it is a false religion. As a matter of fact, Judaism is an essential part of God's ongoing revelation to the human race.

As far as anti-Semitic preaching is concerned, using texts of the New Testament in a way to arouse anti-Semitic feelings is completely abhorrent to the Catholic Church. I must say that, as a boy, I never once heard an anti-Semitic homily or catechesis. For example, I heard, probably as a teenager for the first time, that "the Jews killed Christ." When I was a boy, we were told that the Jews were certainly involved in the death of Christ, as were the Romans, who performed the execution proper. But the nuns or priests always went on to say, "But the truth of the matter is, you and I by our sins, which God knew then and which we still commit at the present moment, were responsible for the death of Christ." Therefore, it was very, very clear that the Jews or the Romans were the *accidental* means, but not the *essential* means, of the death of Christ. So we have to be very careful.

You mention a point which some of our own clergy

do not take seriously enough — that the text, whether that from the Hebrew Bible or the New Testament, is a sacred text and should not be tampered with. For instance, in problematic passages in the Gospel of John, there is mention of "the Jews," and apparently in a negative way.

L.K.: Let us recall the text was written by a fellow Jew.

P.S.: Exactly. Saint John has very interesting ways of presenting what he considers a good form of Judaism and a bad form of Judaism. His hostility toward "the Jews" is directed toward a religious establishment which surely caused difficulties for him, not to say that he didn't cause some problems for them as well! But nonetheless this is not an indictment by John, let alone by the Church, of the whole Jewish people. And I think that's where the role of the preacher is so critical: A text must be explained, and that's the task of the homilist or preacher.

The First Century

L.K.: Our discussion of rabbinic Judaism and early Christianity as reflected in the New Testament points out the need, our urgent need, to study and consider the first century. For many years I didn't want to use the term "first century." I considered it a Christian expression. Now, after much study, I realize (as I said in an earlier chapter) that it was the first century for the Jewish people as well as for early Christianity, because in that first century two branches — and I follow the idea of Saint Paul about Christianity, a branch of Judaism — two branches appeared or came out of the biblical experience. One was rabbinic Judaism, that is, the rabbinic and Pharisaic explanations of the biblical text, and the New Testament.

The first century was indeed a unique moment in Jewish history and the history of humanity. Sometimes the New Testament portrays the time as that of a spiritual desert illuminated by Jesus' ministry. It was a very creative moment that allowed for different movements like the Sadducean (related to the Temple), the Pharisaic, the Essene movements, and early Christianity to flourish in the context of one century. Out of this rich explanation of the biblical experience came two different ways of approaching a covenantal relationship with God: that is, rabbinic Judaism and early Christianity. So I think of the first century as a period that we need to consider and reconsider, in order to understand our present separate and joint testimony of our relationship with God.

P.S.: I think that Saint Paul would agree with what you say in many ways. Certainly, he referred to that moment in history as the "fullness of time." I've always been struck by the fact that, at least from the Christian vantage point, it does not seem an accident that three great cultures were on the horizon at the same time — those of Athens, Rome, and Jerusalem. And for whatever reason, in God's mysterious plan, all of those coalesced at that time, enabling the God-man relationship to take hold in human civilization in ways that would have been unthought-of before that.

When we talk about this first century, Christians, and particularly Catholics, are very interested in the Jewish roots of Christian liturgy. Let me just throw out a couple of topics, and you can pick them up and go with them:

First of all, our Liturgy of the Hours, particularly the morning and the evening prayer of the Church. The Sunday Eucharist, but even the daily Eucharist which is, for

59

us, preeminently the work of sacrifice. And again, for those unfamiliar, the Eucharist is the ritual, sacramental representation of the sacrifice of Christ's passion, death, and resurrection. The idea of sacrifice in Judaism at that time. The influence of the Passover on the structure of Christian liturgy. The Jewish liturgical calendar. We've already touched on the idea of the lectionary. Prayers for the dead. All of those things certainly have a powerful influence in Catholic liturgy. And if we're going to talk about our Catholic roots, we have to go back to that root which is in Judaism.

The Jewish Roots of Liturgy

L.K.: Let us start with the service itself. We pray three times: morning, early afternoon and evening. We do it in the synagogue or many of us, as for example in my own case, in the afternoon and evening by myself. The service is mainly divided into three sections: an introductory section with psalms; the proclamation of our need to bless God, a recitation of the *Shema* — that is, the proclamation of the unity of God; finally, the eighteen Benedictions (the third part), and a conclusion.

P.S.: If I might interrupt at the moment, just for clarification, you say "our need to bless God." Perhaps you could explain that notion of blessing, which for us Catholics has a different connotation.

L.K.: The *Berakhah*, that is, the invitation to bless God, is a prayer of recognition — recognition of God's creation of the world, God's power, God's serenity, and God's election of the Jewish people with a special mission to the world. And after that, we proclaim the unity of God.

P.S.: As you described the basis structure of the daily service, it becomes clear that this is very similar to the structure of our Morning and Evening Prayer, or what we also call Lauds and Vespers. The Liturgy of the Hours *in toto* includes the Office of Readings, Morning Prayer, Midday Prayer, Evening Prayer, and Night Prayer. In the former rites, we actually had seven services throughout the day, in an attempt to keep alive the tradition of the psalm which says, "Seven times every day I praise you." As we began to realize that the seven there was symbolic of constant prayer rather than a magic number, we didn't have a hesitancy about cutting down the number of "hours." Lauds has three psalms or psalm-like productions, a Scripture reading and the Hymn of Zechariah from the Gospel of Luke, concluding with intercessions. Evening prayer has the same basic structure, except that it's the Hymn or Canticle of Mary from the Gospel of Luke; Night Prayer has a similar structure as well. So we can see a great deal of convergence.

The Prayer of the Dead

L.K.: One of the central sections of the daily prayer or liturgy is a recitation of the *Kaddish*. The *Kaddish* is understood by many in our community as a prayer for the dead, though the word itself relates to *kedushah*, to sanctity. The *Kaddish* is a prayer with which we end every service. It is a proclamation of God's greatness. The *Kaddish* is a whole collection of Aramaic adjectives praising God. (The English translation or any other translation is an invention, because what you would be doing in a real translation is to repeat the same words.) Now, you will also find the *Kaddish* at the end of each volume of the Talmud. The custom was to recite *Kaddish*, proclaiming the glory of God, after completing the study of a volume of the Talmud. Then the question is: How is it that it became a prayer "to remember" the dead? This is a medieval development. You might recall that at a certain point of European history in the Middle Ages, death became central in Christian spirituality and literature. Dante's classic is an example of literature stressing the centrality of death. And at that moment, when the Requiem Mass took on great importance in Christian spirituality, the *Kaddish* also was transformed from a song of proclamation of God's greatness into part of the liturgy for the dead. But the prayer itself doesn't have any word related to funerals or dead people. This is an amazing event in the relationship of Christians and Jews, that is, Christian influences on Judaism.

P.S.: When Christians pray for the dead, it's done in the realization that this is an act in continuity with, or in fidelity to, the example of the Maccabees, who take up the collection in order to pay for a sacrifice to be offered on behalf of the dead at the Temple. How does that tradition of Maccabees continue in any way, or did it continue in any way, in mainline Judaism?

L.K.: I would say that in contemporary Jewish life, as well as centuries ago, the sacrifice was replaced by donations. It is customary — my custom — at every anniversary of my daughter Myriam, to give donations to the synagogue, or to organizations dealing with charity or with children. That is my case. I always give to a children's organization, Jewish or Christian, to help children in memory of Myriam.

P.S.: So in other words, once the temple cult evaporated with the destruction of the Temple, another form was devised, in a good sense, to keep alive the notion of a prayer for the dead having some kind of concrete sacrificial form.

L.K.: There is charity as well as study. I would say also that the concept or experience of sacramental sacrifice, after the destruction of the Temple in the year 70 of the Common Era, was replaced by three dimensions of spirituality. That is, the study of the Torah, prayer, and charity.

P.S.: I recently read an article that you wrote on this whole topic of Christian influences on Jewish religious practices; you have given one example of this, Leon, with the *Kaddish*. What others could you summarize from this article for our readers?

Christian Influences on Judaism

L.K.: I see that you are a good reader. I congratulate you. I never knew about Christian influences on Judaism. I had been taught since I was a child that Christians had taken everything from Judaism and then added their own interpretations. But when I went to the Hebrew Union College in Cincinnati, I took a course taught by Dr. Joseph Gutmann, with whom I wrote my thesis for the rabbinate, about Christian influences on Judaism. I couldn't believe my eyes when I read the description of the course. It went against everything I had been taught. But it was a tremendous learning experience, because Dr. Gutmann not only presented the American experience and influences of Christianity on Judaism, but also in the area called *Ash-*

kenaz — Eastern Europe. Now, many customs that we consider related to Moses and the Mount Sinai experience started and were developed sometime during the Middle Ages in Eastern Europe. Some examples are very important. Christian influence in the Jewish life-cycle can be detected in the Bar Mitzvah ceremony. When a boy reaches the age of thirteen, he is welcomed in the synagogue as a mature person and is obligated to all the commandments of Jewish religiosity. No trace of this ceremony, however, can be found in Jewish sources before the thirteenth century. The custom was that on the first *Shabbat* after his thirteenth birthday, the boy was called up for the biblical reading for the first time and read from the Torah scroll, to indicate to the community-at-large that he was now an active member of the religious majority. The custom can be compared to the Christian Confirmation rite, which was performed shortly after Baptism, but in the thirteenth century was deferred to the year of "discretion," interpreted as the age of ten, twelve, or fourteen. So, was there a Christian influence on the Bar Mitzvah celebration?

But by noting influences, I do not indicate syncretism. Quite the contrary. What I want to show is the richness of dialogue and the possibility of sharing the feeling of religiosity and God, and adapting it to our own life. This has been done by Christians, and it has been done by Jews.

P.S.: You mentioned the danger of syncretism, and this is something that we all have to guard against. Sometimes an overactive enthusiasm on the part of well-meaning people ends up doing violence to all traditions concerned. As many people know, in the Catholic Church there are a number of rites. The largest is the Latin or Roman Rite, but there is the Russian Rite, the Greek Rite, the Byzantine, and so on. All of these are different liturgical expressions, and as a Catholic I can go to any one of those churches, find Catholic worship, enter into their experience and appreciate what they do in that liturgical tradition; but it would be very wrong for me to come back to my Roman Rite church and try to incorporate those elements into our Latin Rite. And I think you're probably saying the same thing in regard to Christianity and Judaism. Certainly, there are things that we can appreciate in each other's liturgical or faith tradition in general, but we must be very cautious to preserve the integrity of our own individual religious identity and experience.

L.K.: I agree thoroughly with you. I am always horrified by the possibility of syncretism, but I do feel that as religious people we can share the sense of God, respectful of the differences but aware of our proximity to God. That relates to a phrase of the French-Jewish philosopher Emmanuel Levinas that is very pertinent to our conversation. He said: "The existence of God is sacred history itself, the sacredness of man's relation to man through which God may pass."

Maintaining Liturgical Forms

P.S.: We've been discussing this interchange between Christianity and Judaism. Do you have some thoughts on why Catholicism has seemed to keep, even with tenacity, more of the Jewish liturgical forms than other branches of Christianity?

L.K.: Well, it might show the wisdom of the Catholic Church vis-à-vis its roots! It relates mainly to the fact that early Christianity was very close to the biblical sources and to Pharisaic theology, and for that reason the Church felt and still feels a closeness to the biblical sources and Abraham. The other denominations grew up out of the more "contemporary" experience — that is, the confrontation with Rome and a separation from a specific Church — rather than coming out of the biblical experience. The Hebrew Bible can even be used as a tool to explain that association, but it doesn't show the close relationship to the biblical source as it does with the Roman Catholic Church.

P.S.: When we're looking at the maintenance of Jewish liturgical forms, undoubtedly the centrality of the Eucharist in the life of the Catholic community has to be considered, and therefore the connection between this event and the Jewish Passover, and specifically the notion of sacrifice contained in the Passover that is then preserved in the Christian Eucharist.

L.K.: Excellent thought. The Passover is very important in our liturgical life. I know many Jews who are not religious, who seldom go to synagogue, who practically never pray, but celebrate Passover every year. For them, the celebration of Passover is a way of expressing their Jewish identity. Sometimes I tell them that they celebrate the freedom from Egypt but forget that the source of that freedom is not an historical event but God. And Passover, for a religious person, is the living and reliving of an event — leaving Egypt — but also encountering God. We left Egypt, not because of a liberation movement, but because God was freeing us from slavery toward a freedom of the spirit. For us, Passover is leaving Egypt on our way to receive the Torah at Mount Sinai. Freedom means the exercise of the Ten Commandments and the rabbinic explanation of the Ten Commandments in our everyday life.

Political or Theological Liberation?

P.S.: I think you introduce a point which some people may think is an aside but is quite central to our concerns as Catholics today. As you know, there's been a whole movement known as liberation theology which has taken hold in various quarters, especially in Latin America. It has been, in varying degrees, an attempt to translate the Christ-event and, by extension, Christian liturgy and the entire Catholic Church, into a form of political liberation. And because Jews and Christians — Jews and Catholics, especially — are very historically rooted and connected to the real world, a political liberation is important. It's because we are children of God that we have the right to live in dignity and freedom. But I would appreciate your reflections on either the Passover or the Christ-event being reinterpreted in an almost exclusively this-worldly dimension, with the heavy political overtones.

L.K.: I am very critical of the so-called theology of liberation. I'm not critical of the political efforts of enslaved minorities in Latin America for their liberation or economic advancement. Quite the contrary. I even propose a sort of industrial revolution in Latin America, in order to give work and economic security to the poor.

What I'm very critical of is using the text in a manner which denigrates its original meaning. In a way, the theology of liberation is a contemporary version of the teaching of contempt. Some of the Church Fathers used the biblical text to show that the coming of Jesus ended the

Jewish vocation of God and God's promise, which has been translated into contemporary terms by the theology of liberation.

P.S.: How do you see the "teaching of contempt" presented in liberation theology?

L.K.: This teaching of contempt is clearly stated in Father Gustavo Gutierrez's *Theology of Liberation.* His book is a sort of a *Midrashic* commentary on the Book of Exodus related to the situation of the poor in Latin America. Father Gutierrez, however, doesn't refer to the fact that other minorities are in a delicate situation in Latin America. Perhaps the situation is not as bad as the situation of the poor, but it is equally bad, socially. For example, in Argentina the case of Jews and Protestants who are second-class citizens because the Constitution holds that the official religion of the State is Roman Catholicism, and that the President and Vice-President have to be Catholics. Both groups, Jews and Protestants, feel like minorities deprived of certain rights. Why hasn't Gutierrez been aware of these other social problems related to the Latin American situation? Why use the Book of Exodus when he could be using other texts, mainly from the New Testament, showing the critical situation of the poor? The other question is: Is it only with a social revolution that one can improve the situation of the poor in Latin America? I have my great doubts, especially coming from that part of the world. What they need is a real industrial revolution because those countries are still in a mercantalist society or a pre-industrial situation.

P.S.: Perhaps the point to highlight here is that, while his concern about the rights and the condition of the poor are legitimate concerns (and one need not be involved with every form of liberation of every group in society), what I find offensive is the attempt to take an event in a text and to use it in ways that the original persons involved would never recognize. And it seems that this is done very frequently, not only with the Passover event itself and with the Book of Exodus, but with theological principles in general. For example, it's not uncommon for feminist theologians to take Mary's Canticle from the Gospel of Luke and suggest that this was a charter of feminist liberation as well. I would like your reflections and reactions to that phenomenon.

L.K.: You mentioned a specific example of the New Testament and a feminist reading of the text. Your criticism does not mean that you are against women's rights, but what you are against — and what I'm also very critical of — is using the text for other purposes.

This is shown in a recent book published in the United States, a commentary on the Book of Job, also by Gustavo Gutierrez. I wrote to the Peruvian priest to share with him my concerns about his use of the Book of Exodus. He never answered me — which was essentially an answer — but in his commentary on Job, he tried to show his concern for the situation of the Jews in the world. In his explanation, he said that the Book of Job and the suffering of Job relate to two contemporary events. One is the Holocaust, and the other the situation of the poor in Latin America, which he puts at the same level. I resent this comment. The difference is tremendous. Jews had no way of escaping the Nazis unless they were hidden by Christian families, or hid themselves in the woods. Anybody who was born a Jew was destined to be murdered. In the case of the poor in Latin America, there are other possibilities: social change, an industrial revolution, new sources of income, etc. The poor are not condemned to be poor; there are possibilities for change. The main thing is for the leadership to understand that change should become a reality in each nation.

P.S.: You may be aware that part of the reason for Gutierrez's change — distancing himself somewhat from some of the more objectionable forms of liberation theology — is that his own bishop had disciplined him, and one of the conditions for returning to the exercise of his priestly ministry was to take a second look at his more extreme positions in that first book. Perhaps now that we've dealt with that issue, we can return to a more pristine discussion of the Passover ritual itself, what it meant then, what it means now, and then to connect that specifically with the Christian understanding of the Eucharist as our Passover.

Chapter Four

Celebrating the Liturgy

Passover and Memory

L.K.: Passover is an experience of exile and return. The Jewish person feels that in the time of Passover he or she is going through an experience of the desert and an encounter with God. For that reason, the house becomes that place of awesome contact with God as it can be experienced in the desert.

P.S.: You highlight a point which is very crucial, I think, for a healthy understanding of liturgy — the role of memory. So many people — Catholics included — misunderstand that, for example, what we are attempting to do in the celebration of the Eucharist is to remember an event, not in a past sense, but rather as a sacred memory that leads to sacred reality. And if I understand you and Jewish liturgy correctly, Jews celebrating the Passover do not look upon it as merely an event of the past, but rather an event of the past which is brought into the present, so that they *are* in the desert, they *are* on Mount Sinai; at that very moment the action of the past is being recreated for them.

L.K.: You sound so Jewish, Peter. That's exactly the point. It is the experience of *zikaron* — that is, remembrance. The ritual of Passover points out the need to remember and to share that memory with the children and

71

the family. So we remember the Passover by preparing the house for that moment of the reading of the *Haggadah*, the liturgy for Passover, but also to have the sense that life that week is not going to be the same as existence the rest of the year. We relive the desert experience, the exile of slavery, and the return to the Promised Land, to God, and to a covenantal living every day of our existence.

As I said before, it is customary, and my wife Myra and I do this at home: clean the whole house from anything that might have a leavened product, so the house is prepared for Passover. And I want to point out that every year a week before the cleaning, my Catholic neighbor reminds me that in her basement there is a place for all the leavened products of our house. So once we've cleaned the house we take down the dishes that we used during the year, the leavened products, and other articles that are related to the rest of the year. Everything is "new" at Passover — china, forks, spoons, food, etc.

P.S.: Christians should immediately connect this with Saint Paul's reminder that because of the Resurrection of Christ, we have to throw out all of the old leavened products — that we are now, as it were, a "new creation." Everything is brand new. And if we understand our own celebration of the Eucharist in the context of this primal religious event of the Passover, a great deal comes into focus much more clearly.

You also mentioned, Leon, that in a sense at the time of the Passover and for worship generally, the believer steps outside of time, and enters into past, present and future, which in theological language is eternity. I think some religious people who try to be "contemporary" fail to understand the necessity of that stepping outside the normal sphere of human events, for liturgy is intended to be a different mode of existence; if we simply take into liturgy everything that we are and do normally, whether it's our music or language or style of dress, we cheat ourselves out of the experience of the eternal.

L.K.: The Egyptian experience reflected in the Passover celebration is an event that is common for us in different moments of history. For example, the destruction of the First and Second Temples, the expulsion from Spain, the expulsion from European cities, or the Holocaust are reminders that the Egyptian slavery, independently of Egypt itself, is a reality in our history. And in Passover we feel that we are in history and outside history, that we remember not only one moment of exile, but other moments of exile through more than 5,000 years of history. So Passover for us is a lesson of history, but beyond history. We are in an eternal covenant with God, witnessing to God, and facing the challenges of history. We remember the Egyptian slavery, but we also have a prayer for the Holocaust and the people who were murdered during the Nazi domination.

P.S.: You're touching on points which are essential for Catholics. As you may know, certain fundamentalist Christians accuse Catholics of attempting a blasphemous reenactment of Christ's Last Supper and death on Calvary. Our response is, "By no means are we attempting to recreate that past event, but the liturgical reenactment of the event reinserts us into that moment, from which we then draw strength to live our contemporary lives." And as I listen to your description of a theology of the liturgy of the Passover, it becomes clear that we're on the very same track in that regard.

L.K.: Passover is a very personal experience in the life of every Jewish family. Myra and I have prepared a special liturgy for that celebration, and we hope that one Passover you will come to our home, because we always invite our Christian friends to share the Passover meal. And in that liturgy (the *Haggadah*) we respected the Hebrew text itself, but a translation was made in a way to reflect the contemporary sense of exile and return. In our century, we have experienced that through the horror of the Holocaust and the return to the Promised Land by the creation of the State of Israel. And every Passover, I always recall and sometimes mention to the people attending our Passover dinner, my own memory of Passover 1945.

We were in Argentina and the news stories were coming about what happened in Europe, but we didn't know the whole horror of the Holocaust. We still believed that members of my family and other families had survived. We didn't know anything. But news stories were coming. And I remember my father — we were the four of us, my mother, my brother, my father and I — reciting the *Haggadah*. And suddenly my father put the text down, got up, raised his hand against the ceiling, and started screaming at God, "God, why did you treat us this way? Why did you let the Nazis destroy our people? Haven't we followed your commandments?" He was furious, screaming, and my mother tried to quiet him down, to no avail. My brother and I looked at each other; we never saw my father like that, screaming and crying. And then my father stopped and continued the reading of the *Haggadah*. The next day, he asked us what we studied in Hebrew school. The point is that despite history we had to continue with our tradition. And I had the same experience at the death of my daughter Myriam. I did the same thing as my father, but later on I realized that I had to continue with my commitment because of the communion with God and my obligations to my family and my people.

Eight Days of Celebration

P.S.: I should underscore for our readers what is certainly obvious to many, but not to all, that the Passover is a home celebration rather than for a synagogue.

L.K.: Some synagogues have family celebrations, but during the week, not the first night.

P.S.: How long is the Passover celebration and, aside from the first-night dinner, what else goes into the observance of the feast?

L.K.: Well, there is a second-night celebration and also the last two days. Outside Israel it's an eight-day celebration, and in Israel it's a seven-day celebration. This is due to the fact that in antiquity the rabbis added a day to certain celebrations because of distance. They didn't have the phone, the fax or radar as in our days. So in order to avoid problems, they would add a day, with the exception of *Yom Kippur*, because that would mean two days of fast.

During Passover we observe certain food obligations. We eat *matzo*, the bread of affliction, which doesn't have any leaven — we don't eat anything that has leaven — and we try to eat fish and other kinds of food that would relate to an experience of exile and the desert. Sometimes I feel, and perhaps you can enlighten me about it, that the *matzo* sounds or looks like the Host.

P.S.: Actually, several points came across. First of all, Catholics hearing about the eight-day feast would automatically think of our octave feasts in Catholicism. In the old days there were many octave feasts but with the revision of our liturgical calendar in the '70s that has been reduced to the two principal feasts of Christianity, Christmas and Easter. These are celebrated for eight days; the first and the last days of the feasts are the big celebrations, with smaller observances throughout the week. Liturgically, for instance, the Christmas and Easter octaves would have the same solemnity attached to each Mass as there would be for the first day of the feast. When you were mentioning the *matzo*, immediately it clicked, of course, that it is by deliberate design that the bread used in the Eucharist for the Latin Rite (but not generally for the Eastern Rites) is unleavened bread. The Eastern Rites, interestingly enough, deliberately use leavened bread because of Paul's idea of the Resurrection of Christ and the connection with the Eucharist; thus they use raised dough. In the Latin Rite there was interest in maintaining the connection with Judaism and the Passover.

A Year's Observance

P.S.: Leon, you've talked about the meaning of Passover in the Jewish calendar. What other liturgical feasts are celebrated, and where and how?

L.K.: The liturgical calendar is central in our religious life. I would say that our "way" is around days and months related to the covenantal relationship. There is a time, a weekly time, when everything stops. That is the *Shabbat*, a day of total rest and also of spiritual recovery. On that day, as we celebrate the creation and re-creation of the world in accordance with rabbinic thought, we devote the twenty-four hours to a renewal of our relationship with God.

Certain festivals reflect specific aspects of the relationship with God. Let's take, for example, two central days of the Jewish calendar. One is *Rosh Hashanah*, and the second, *Yom Kippur*. *Rosh Hashanah* is more than a new year. It is a time of renewal in the covenantal relationship between God and Israel. At *Rosh Hashanah*, we make an account of the past year, looking hopefully for the new year to come, but essentially it's a reckoning of the soul. And that reckoning of the soul is done in the ten days between *Rosh Hashanah* and *Yom Kippur*. In *Yom Kippur* we confess our transgressions, but we also renew our spiritual life. *Yom Kippur* is not only an occasion for forgiveness by God but also, and very importantly in our spirituality, for mutual forgiveness. The liturgy says that if we don't forgive each other for our transgressions and ill behavior, God takes a long, long time to forgive us.

Other festivals commemorate specific moments of our relationship with God. One is *Hanukkah*, which has become very popular, especially in the United States. *Hanukkah* recalls the fight for the right to be different centuries ago under the domination of the Hellenistic powers in the Middle East. Those powers wanted to impose the Greek way of life and thinking upon religious groups in the Middle East, but Israel reacted and fought back, winning the freedom of conscience that allowed them to build the Second Temple and to develop Judaism in the rabbinical sense of the word.

P.S.: Why is *Hanukkah* more observed in the States than elsewhere?

L.K.: *Hanukkah* in the United States is much more commemorated than in Latin America or in Europe, where it is a rather minor festival, though it's related to other moments of our history like, for example, the Second World War. But in the United States, because of the importance of the Christmas celebration, *Hanukkah* has become very special in family life. In *Hanukkah*, every day children get a present; thus they cannot complain that their Christian neighbors are getting more presents than they. I recall only that when I was young, my father would give us one present the first day of *Hanukkah* and that was the end of "the good life."

P.S.: Do you want to explain the origins of the *menorah*, which people see in great evidence and even in public displays at the time of *Hanukkah*?

L.K.: That relates to the Temple. The Temple was desecrated by the Hellenists, and when the Maccabees took over Jerusalem, they had very little clean oil to use in a *menorah*, or candelabrum of seven branches. The oil lasted for seven days, which is part of the commemoration of the *Hanukkah* miracle, that the light of religious freedom lasted for a week, reminding the community of the obligation to fight for religious rights, especially the right to be different spiritually.

Another festival is the *Shavuoth*, or the Feast of Weeks, related to a revelation and the giving of the Ten Commandments. The other celebration is *Sukkoth*, the Festival of Tabernacles, when we are obligated to eat at least one meal in a *sukkah*, built in the back of the house or in a balcony, to remind the Jewish people of the days of the desert — that is, the days when we prepared ourselves to return to the Promised Land after the slavery in Egypt. The *sukkah* reminds the Jewish person of the obligation to be humble and to be grateful to God for all the goodness that we receive every day, and that many times we take for granted.

I recall that one of our great theologians, Franz Rosenzweig, referred many times in his correspondence with Martin Buber to the centrality of the calendar in Jewish religious life. The calendar is not an account of days and weeks, but the calendar allows a glimpse into the peculiar life of the individual and the community and the ongoing process of knowing God and consolidating the covenantal relationship. I wonder if something similar exists in the Christian Faith.

The Christian Calendar

P.S.: The calendar is critically important for Christians. When I say "for Christians" I am speaking of those who have a liturgical tradition; therefore, Catholics, Eastern Orthodox, Anglicans and Lutherans, and increasingly other mainline Protestant denominations who have recaptured both a liturgical sense and, with that, the notion of a liturgical calendar. What I am saying at the moment will reflect most clearly Catholic and Eastern Orthodox approaches to worship times and seasons.

The primary feast for Christians is Sunday. Now when most people hear "feast" they tend to think of a particular day like Christmas or Easter. But in fact, the early Christians (for probably three centuries at least) did not have a liturgical calendar in the sense that we are familiar with it. And so, Sunday was for them the transferred Lord's Day of the Jewish *Shabbat*, and done to commemorate the Resurrection of Christ from the dead. As

79

time went on, plugging into the Jewish roots, and more comfortable in doing so with distance from early problems within Judaism, the Christian community decided to incorporate a much more structured calendar. Therefore, Easter itself was the central feast of Christianity, which it still is today. As you may know, there was a conflict in the Early Church between the Eastern Church and the Church of Rome on the question of the date of Easter, with the Roman idea being to keep it much more closely tied to the celebration of Passover. Interestingly, too, it was the Roman decision to keep unleavened bread for the Eucharist, whereas the Church of the East uses leavened bread, as I mentioned before.

Within that overall liturgical celebration of Easter, we would have to tie in with it a triduum: beginning on Holy Thursday of Holy Week, the night on which Jesus celebrated the Last Supper, His last Passover, with His disciples; Good Friday, the commemoration of His death; Holy Saturday, His time in the tomb; then the biggest liturgical event of Christian life, the celebration of the Easter Vigil on Holy Saturday night. In the Early Church, that liturgy extended from the nighttime of Holy Saturday all the way through dawn of Easter morning. We have a much more modified approach to that now.

L.K.: What other feasts are celebrated?

P.S.: Next in significance would be the cycle of Advent and Christmas, celebrating the birth of Jesus and the four weeks prior to that of penitential but joyful anticipation of His birth. The preparation for the Easter season is the six weeks, or forty days, of Lent. Like Judaism, Christianity is very fond of the number forty for times of preparation and anticipation and so forth. Fifty days after Easter is the celebration of Pentecost, which is the Christian celebration of the Jewish Feast of Weeks. And then inserted throughout would be what we refer to as the Sanctoral Cycle, which celebrates the passion, death and resurrection of Jesus in the lives of the saints, those who exemplify particular qualities related to the life and teaching of Jesus.

Passover and Easter

L.K.: One of the areas that requires our joint examination and even reflection is the time of Passover and Easter. You referred to the Last Supper as a Passover meal. There is a tendency in contemporary scholarship, both Christian and Jewish, to consider the Last Supper not necessarily a Passover meal, but rather a reunion of Jesus and His disciples sharing bread. If we consider the Last Supper as a Passover meal the symbolism of that event becomes very interesting, especially in relationship to the idea of total exile and return, which is part of the Jewish tradition. It also relates to messianic and mystical interpretations that were current in the first century and that call for our joint examination. Otherwise, I'm always concerned that our sharing of festivals, especially those dating from the first century, might take us to syncretism. This syncretism can become a reality in joint prayer today, or in the analysis of the first century.

P.S.: When you talk about questions regarding the Last Supper being or not being a Passover meal, some readers may know that there is certainly a question in the New Testament itself. The Synoptic Gospels — the Gospels according to Matthew, Mark and Luke — are

81

very clear about the fact that this is a Passover meal. John, on the other hand, tells us that at the hour of the Last Supper the lambs were being slaughtered in the Temple. Obviously, there is some kind of a question. Now that's resolved in a variety of ways. One is to say that Jesus was, perhaps, following an Essene calendar, which was a few days off from that of Temple Judaism. Another possibility is to say that He Who felt quite comfortable in exceeding the Law in certain instances simply "anticipated" the Passover supper, knowing that He would die the next day, and therefore wanting to celebrate this with the disciples. So it certainly is a controverted question, even within Christianity, although I venture to say that most of the Christian readers of this book will be hearing this for the first time.

L.K.: What you said, Peter, reminds me of a present trend in Jewish scholarship concerning the first centuries, especially at the Hebrew University in Jerusalem. Professor David Flusser wrote several studies showing the importance of the study of the Gospels and the New Testament in order to understand the state and development of rabbinic Judaism in the days of Jesus.

The Three Branches

P.S.: I think it would be of interest to Christians to know the place of Hebrew in the Jewish liturgy at the present moment. Perhaps you could give us an overview of the three branches of Judaism, because I'm sure it differs greatly from one to another.

L.K.: Hebrew is central in prayer and study. There is, however, the reality that many Jews do not know Hebrew well, or repeat prayers even though they don't know their meaning. I strongly recommend that friends and, when I had a congregation, my congregants study Hebrew in order to be immersed in the spirit of the Bible and the relationship with God. Hebrew is a very special language, economical in its terminology, with very few adjectives but many, many nouns. That makes translation quite difficult. Sometimes at services I read the English translation, and I realize that the translator is a rather non-poetic soul, because of the ways he or she translates the original Hebrew. The translation is like a razor; one can hurt himself very easily. But I do realize that many people want to follow the service and need that translation in order to understand what is going on.

Hebrew is fundamental in Orthodox communities. There would be one or two readings in English — namely, a psalm or a prayer for the welfare of the president of the state or a prayer for somebody who is ill, but the main emphasis is Hebrew. The Conservative movement will use Hebrew during the service but also English translations of many prayers. The Reform movement originally focused on English, but the new version of the Reform prayer book emphasizes the use of Hebrew and asks the congregation to use more Hebrew during the prayer.

I imagine that something similar is the case in the Catholic Church. I know, Peter, that you have been somewhat critical about some translations of sacred texts.

P.S.: The question of a sacred language is also important in Catholicism. In the Latin Rite, or Western Church, as the name suggests the primary language was and still is Latin. Now in the United States the importance of Latin is noted more in the breach than in the observance. As you travel in Europe and even in Asia or Africa it would not be at all uncommon for a priest to use the vernacular — that is, the language of the people of an area, in tandem with Latin. In Germany, for example, the prayer books in the pews of any congregation are bilingual for all practical purposes; the priest will move very easily from reciting a prayer in German to chanting a prayer in Latin. Certainly the Second Vatican Council opened the doors to a wider use of the vernacular, but never envisioned jettisoning Latin. And although I have a great love for Latin in general and Gregorian chant in particular, I believe that there is a value and a good place for the use of vernacular. You allude to my campaign of late to improve our translations, and indeed we have some generally horrendous translations. The Italians have a proverb which charges that every translator is a traitor, and there's more truth than poetry to that proverb, I think. And so it's important for us to try to recapture some of the sense of the sacred even in the use of the vernacular. But I do find it interesting that even reform Jews have attempted to get more in touch with their roots, precisely by using Hebrew more frequently in their own liturgy. Among Catholics in America there seems to be an interest among the younger clergy and the younger, better educated lay Catholics to try to recapture some of what was perhaps thrown out too quickly.

Translation and Treason

L.K.: You referred to that Italian saying about translation and treason. This is a very serious concern for me. I have been reading some liturgies in which words have been carefully avoided because they were either in the masculine or in the feminine forms. The language becomes so "clean" that one cannot feel that it is part of the religious tradition. I remember many years ago translating a prayer book into Spanish and trying to avoid any reference to God as the King. Living under a political dictatorship, I felt that I had to use another kind of language. So, in the prayer that we bless God as "King of the universe" I used the term "ground of being" (under the influence of Paul Tillich). I gave my father a copy of the book. He was proud of his son's work, but he pointed out to me, when he read that translation, that he was a little bit uneasy about the terminology. He looked at me and he said, "King or not king, did you pray this morning?" And I feel that his non-sophisticated but deeply religious approach is a reminder to us to be careful in the way we deal with sacred languages.

P.S.: You hit on a very sensitive nerve within the Catholic community in the United States. There is a desire on the part of a very small but intensely vocal minority to ensure that we use "politically correct" language. First of all, the concerns of this group are by no means the concerns of any sizable portion of the Catholic community. But over and above that, by this drive or campaign we find ourselves politicizing two of the most important things in life — namely, language and worship. Therefore a person's status or suitability is determined on the basis of the kind of language that he uses. And so, we go through a linguistic cleansing, which is every bit as offensive as the "ethnic cleansing" that we hear so much about as well. Therefore, I think it's important for those of us who understand the nature of the sacred, and how language is a reflection of the sacred, to ensure that the language we use does indeed reflect the beauty and majesty of God.

As you know, Leon, we are in the process of receiving a new catechism for the Catholic Church, and coincidentally the breakdown that you and I have followed in this book is exactly the breakdown of the new catechism — namely, doctrine, liturgy, and moral life. Thus what we Christians and Jews believe, we celebrate in the liturgy, and the liturgy gives us the wherewithal to pursue this in terms of leading a godly life, which, of course, is our next concern.

Chapter Five

Leading the Moral Life

The Ten Suggestions?

P.S.: I'm sure that when people hear us refer to the moral life, immediately the Ten Commandments come to mind. Under the influence of the '60s, many people began looking on the Ten Commandments in a very negative way. First of all, because the majority of the commandments are framed in negative terminology. And, secondly, due to modern psychology of a bad sort, the commandments came to be seen more as suggestions than anything else. And it's interesting that traditional Catholic theology and traditional Jewish theology would be quite aligned with each other on two basic notions. First, that the commandments do have relevance today, and second, the standing of the commandments, which makes them a part of someone's lived experience of life, rather than some kind of imposition of a capricious deity.

L.K.: The Ten Commandments are fundamental in Jewish religiosity. But they require an expounding of the basic meaning of the text; this has been the work of interpretation of the rabbis and our teachers. In different rabbinic commentaries, or works of theology, the rabbis have pointed out the nature of each commandment vis-à-vis specific moments of the life of the individual. So the Ten Commandments are not an end in themselves; they are a means by which to implement the relationship with God. I feel that the Ten Commandments require a rethinking vis-à-vis this moment of our life. Especially I have in consideration the two historical events that changed the rhythm of our spiritual life — the Holocaust, and the establishment of the State of Israel. To this, in the United States, we have to add the American Jewish experience that is a unique moment in the history of our people.

So the Ten Commandments require for our understanding an "expanding" in terms of the everyday life of an individual.

It is important to point out, as part of our Jewish-Christian relationship, that the Ten Commandments do not play in our liturgy the importance that they play in Christian liturgy and spirituality. This is related to the time of confrontation between Judaism and Christianity. Because of the emphasis on the Ten Commandments in Christian liturgy, medieval Judaism decided not to include the Decalogue in our liturgy, so as not to convey the possibility of a Christian influence. This is part of our history, that might not have any importance in our days.

P.S.: The commandments are not used in Catholic liturgy or Eastern Orthodox liturgy, but interestingly enough they are used in various Protestant liturgical services, and that's surely the case in the traditional Anglican rite. But they would hold a central place in Catholic catechesis, which is the training of people in the Faith, and they would be memorized by Catholic children from second grade on. They would also form a part of one's examination of conscience prior to receiving the Sacrament of Penance — that is, going to confession.

Applying the Commandments

L.K.: Let us reflect on each one of the command-ments in relationship to our present life. The first one refers to the obligation to honor one God — that is, the God of Sinai, in rabbinic Judaism. Today this concept is under consideration in much of our theological research — that is, a search for a new concept of God. "New concept of God" does not mean a new terminology, or a terminol-ogy that might be appealing to the new generations. A "new concept of God" means an understanding of God's call and God's Word at this precise moment of our history when we have gone through total exile, the death of Auschwitz and the recovery, the return to the Promised Land, and the creativity of Jewish life in other parts of the world. Many of our theologians are working in this area, and we need to understand God's voice at the end of the twentieth century. This does not mean to deny God, but to understand God's Word and God's call.

P.S.: In the Catholic approach to the First Command-ment, we see it as the importance of affirming monotheism, which, of course, would be a point that might be questioned by some Jews, inasmuch as they could see Jesus "usurping," for Christians, the sovereignty or the omnipotence of God. But as we explained in our first chapter, the Trinity, properly understood in the most care-ful theological way, does not compromise the unity of God. This commandment would also contain within it prohibitions against idols of any kind: so often people smirk at the silly Hebrews fashioning a golden calf, but they don't realize that there are the contemporary gods of money and sex and power. Therefore, we would say that any thing or any person which occupies the place of God or pushes God from the center stage of one's life is, by that definition, an idol.

L.K.: The Second Commandment talks about not misusing the name of God. This is important in reference to a problem that I consider extremely serious in religious life — that is, the political appropriation of God's name. In the name of God, politicians or political groups have advocated lack of rights, even persecution, or a sort of ideology that has hurt religious life in the long run. That doesn't mean that we should be outside politics or not project our religiosity into the political arena. What I distrust is using the name of God and theological thought as an ideology, rather than a means to convey the covenantal relationship and its morality.

P.S.: The Second Commandment for us is very closely tied to the Jewish understanding of the sacredness of God's name, and how important it is not to use the name casually, let alone as a curse or in a negative context. Very often people have a tendency to use the name of God lightly; we even had that film, *Oh, God*, which in many ways was nothing more than a comedy, and yet the name of God was consistently used in that way. For us, it would also include the importance attached to the name of Jesus, coming from the Hebrew, which means "God saves." I always remind Catholics that the name of God is so sacred to Jews that they do not use the word, *"Yahweh."* Unfortunately, in some of the more contemporary approaches to Catholic life, the word is thrown around all over; some Christians even suppose they're throwing across a bridge to Judaism, when in point of fact it's an action that would be abhorrent.

L.K.: The Third Commandment talks about keeping holy the Sabbath. Earlier, I referred to the centrality of the *Shabbat* in Jewish spirituality. But the text points out the need to "keep holy," rather than to keep the *Shabbat* only as a day of rest. This conveys the need to make that day one entirely devoted to inner life, to pray in the synagogue, to study in the afternoon the biblical portion of the week, and to recuperate from a week of struggle, of confrontation with neighbors or friends, from a week of toil. The *Shabbat* is not a day of idleness, but it is a day devoted to inner work — that is, a cleansing of the heart in the relationship with God and oneself. I wonder if this spirit of the *Shabbat* is projected into the Sunday celebrated by Christians.

P.S.: Thirty years ago the Jewish notion of the Sabbath rest was intensely lived in the Catholic community of my boyhood. We began the day with Sunday Mass. There would be a family breakfast — a very big, important breakfast. There would be various family activities and a large Sunday afternoon dinner. The family would go to church again on Sunday afternoon for Vespers. But gradually, under the influence of modernity and in making concessions to modernity, the Sunday observance for most American Catholics has become nonexistent. Many who go to Mass consider that they have by that very action indeed fulfilled the Third Commandment. The law of God and the law of the Church still forbid what theologians call "servile work," but again, the average Catholic tends to use Sunday to go shopping, to do laundry, to cut the grass; it's a catch-up day. This is something that's most regrettable, and unfortunately, is not usually handled either through catechesis or through preaching. I am unaware of any priest of my acquaintance who has addressed that problem for even a moment in a homily over the last ten or fifteen years.

L.K.: I deeply appreciate the fact that you refer to modernity. It's a word that I was looking for, and you were kind enough to enter it into our conversation. This idea about modernity relates to the Fourth Commandment that enjoins us to honor our father and mother. We are living in a time of tremendous transformation. When I look back into the past, I realize that in my relationship with my father and mother, I behaved in a way that was completely different from the way my children relate to me.

There was in my youth the concept that father and mother were sacred entities that were beyond any criticism or comment. Their word was the last word. But I lived with a different position, in which my children disagreed with me, but disagreed with full respect. What I cannot accept is the fact that I now see many families in which the children disagree with their parents without any respect. The parents are only the means to get money for vacations or similar matters. But the basic relationship that makes of a family that creative nucleus, which changes spiritually the life of children and projects a message of peace to society, is lost because of the tremendous changes that have come with modernity. Personally, I do not want to go back to the past, to the way I related to my parents. It was another period in life, and of course in another country, in a family deeply influenced by Eastern European standards. I developed with my own children a different relationship in which I am still the father, but I'm not a dictator. I'm their father, a source of authority and knowledge, but not of totalitarian authority and knowledge, and that makes a great difference.

P.S.: I agree with everything that you mentioned, and if we're going to consider what modernity has done, both to the Sabbath observance and to respect for parents, the one thing that horrifies me is how so many American children feel quite comfortable in exiling their parents to nursing homes and senior citizen villages, which to Europeans or Asians or Africans who come here is a source of great shock and dismay when they discover that for the first time.

The Fifth Commandment forbids one to kill. You already alluded to that, and I always explain to people that actually the Hebrew word contains within itself the notion of malicious killing or murder. And so there is a justifiable defense of one's life; thus neither self-defense nor a just war would come under the prohibition of the Fifth Commandment. We would also consider here any taking of innocent human life, as well as suicide, activities that would tend to diminish the quality of life of people, and fighting and contentiousness, all of which lead to murder.

Different Aspects of Two Commandments

L.K.: Let's turn our attention to commandments six and nine. Six says, "Thou shalt not commit adultery," and nine says, "Thou shalt not covet thy neighbor's wife." One can ask, "Why has the biblical text repeated what seems to be the same transgression?" I feel that the Bible is wiser than contemporary readers, because both commandments refer to different aspects of coveting. One is the fact of not committing adultery. Marriage is a sacred enterprise, in which man and woman together are building up not only a

93

family but a creation. In a way, they are recreating the world. In our wedding liturgy, we refer to the need for the couple to build and rebuild life, not only by having children, but also by a process of personal change, of respect for each other because that special, sacred union goes beyond intimacy into the realm of creativity. For that reason, adultery is not only a lack of respect for the other person in the marriage — a form of denigration of the other person — but also an insult to creativity, to God's command to create and re-create life by the lives of two persons.

P.S.: You know, Leon, as you were expounding on the Sixth and Ninth Commandments, I started to smile, because I thought I was hearing Pope John Paul II talk.

L.K.: Well, there is no doubt both of us are of Polish origins.

P.S.: I think it's also the influence of Saint John of the Cross on both of you, too. But what you were saying reflects his philosophy of personalism. So often people look on the commandments in a burdensome way. I referred earlier to external constraints, whereas John Paul's approach to Christian morality, which is just biblical morality for all practical purposes, is to say: God has not given us commandments to show that He's in charge, which obviously He can do as the sovereign Lord; rather, to break a commandment is wrong, not because it's a law, but the law exists because it's bad to do, especially to oneself. And when you were reflecting on the whole sexual question, you were making the point which is so important to appreciate, particularly for young people who are being formed in their attitudes toward the tremendous gift of sexuality, that this is a question of personal dignity. And, yes, our dignity is offended and even destroyed by casual sexual contact.

From the General to the Specific

L.K.: There are two other commandments that I feel are related. Those are numbers seven and ten. Seven says, "Thou shalt not steal," and number ten says, "Thou shalt not covet thy neighbor's goods." I think that these two commandments follow the same criteria of six and nine. One of them talks in general, and the other in the particular case. Number seven stresses the question of stealing, a wide meaning. It is not only the act of stealing something that belongs to another person, but according to the rabbis it is also the lack of economic respect for the other person. For example, the rabbis emphasize, based in the biblical tradition, the need to pay regularly the salary of each person. It should be done at a certain point of time, day or night, and the obligation is to do it always at a certain time, so the person can use that money for himself or his family. Number ten criticizes a special dimension of human nature — that we are so jealous of the other's properties, or what they have or can have, that sometimes we forget the goodness we have. We would like to have more coats than we need, or more shoes than we need, because our neighbor dresses much better than we do. But what we forget is that at least we are fortunate enough to be dressed for winter or to be well shod.

I do feel, however, that here I'm addressing an ideological or a political matter. Some people, even theologians, feel that coveting is part of a system that allows economic transformation and the growth of that economy. Others emphasize the goodness of capitalism as the only way of general comfort and economic growth. I feel, personally, though I'm not overly enthusiastic or critical of capitalism, that we need to have a prudent approach to that system.

P.S.: I agree with you wholeheartedly. The Catholic approach to material things — let alone materialism — is in many ways to say in reference to communism or socialism or capitalism: A plague on all your houses. What is sacrosanct is the person and the dignity of the person, and when things start to occupy the place which belongs to a human being, we are already involved in breaking a number of commandments all at the same time — idol worship and coveting and, eventually, stealing.

A Reverence for Truth

L.K.: And this takes us to the last commandment that we want to comment on, the eighth, "Thou shalt not bear false witness against thy neighbor." False witness, generally, is not only for judicial cases, but also in everyday life. Gossiping, criticizing other people, or repeating racist comments are part of that false witness against a neighbor that hurts the human relationship and opens the door to social and racial confrontation. It is so wise that the commandment uses the noun, "witness," because witnessing is part of our relationship with God, by which we implement daily God's commandment and God's Word. If we are a witness, we have to respect the other person of God also as a witness.

P.S.: This commandment calls us to have a reverence for the truth. Saint Thomas Aquinas said, of all of the sins which men commit, the one that is the most heinous in God's eyes is lying, because it destroys any possibility for human communication. It denies the dignity of the person, who is supposed to be a truth-teller by nature. It denies the possibility that anyone could ever trust the communication of another person once we know that person has told a lie. And unfortunately, truth-telling is in rather short supply in our society. We see it in politics, we see it in economics, we see it even in family relationships.

L.K.: Indeed, the Ten Commandments are a source of reflection for both of our faith communities, but especially for us Jews and Christians in our relationship with and in our witnessing to the world.

P.S.: I think what you said, Leon, has very serious implications for both Jews and Christians in terms of the understanding and living of biblical morality. And inasmuch as you represent Judaism and serve as the elder brother in this relationship, maybe you could kick off our next topic with some reflections on what we really mean when we speak of a biblical approach to the moral life?

Grounded in the Bible

L.K.: When we Jews talk about dimensions of biblical morality, we refer not only to the biblical text itself, but also to the expounding of the meaning of the text that was done by the rabbis and our teachers. One example comes to my mind very vividly. I remember reading in one of Martin Buber's books about his conversation with a theologian in Germany. The theologian was criticizing the biblical God who was asking Israel to destroy a whole people on their way to the Promised Land, or to perform

97

their religious duties. Martin Buber was saddened for a while, and then said, "Perhaps the biblical writer or the biblical person didn't hear the exact Word of God." Buber was trying to stress the fact that the Bible is primary in our spirituality, but it is an experience that must be actualized in our lives. Perhaps the biblical person didn't hear God well, but our duty is to listen to that Word of God and to make it a reality in our own lives. That's what the rabbis did through the *Midrash*, the literary explanation of the Bible that was very well known to Jesus, and the *Mishnah*, the religious implementation of ritual and prayer. There is a biblical morality that I have to actualize in my present experience. The main concepts for me are the sacredness of creation, the sacredness of life, and the sacredness of human relationships. However, the sacredness relates, according to our teachings, to the special circumstances that the reader of the Bible is going through. For that reason, for us the explanation of the text in terms of the covenantal relationship is so important.

P.S.: When we look at the idea of a biblical morality, we consider first of all the importance of God's Word in the past, and as you suggest, God's Word to us in the present. But that Word is a mediated Word. It's not immediate to us, certainly not today. And it's mediated to us by the circumstances of our lives; for us Catholics, it's mediated in a particular way through the Church's magisterium, which corresponds to your notion of an explanation of text. Even Martin Luther, who was a great devoté of "*Sola Scriptura*" — Scripture alone — recognized the fact that Scripture in and of itself didn't provide all the answers to human life. He made the quip at one point that using Scripture alone he could prove that beer was better than wine. And so, when we speak about a biblical morality, we're not talking about using the Bible as a kind of dictionary to look up a problem to see what the answer is, and simply take it wholesale into the present. If that were the case, of course, we would have no answers to most of the major ethical questions of contemporary life, simply because the problems didn't exist in the time of the biblical authors.

L.K.: And that's an invitation to humility. I know that humility is not easy in our days, but it's very important in regard to the biblical text. We cannot hold our contemporary "spiritual superiority" over the biblical text. It is a *hutzpa* that will hurt us in the final analysis. The Bible is a sacred text that is open to interpretation, and we must have the implementation of that interpretation in our everyday lives. When we turn to the Bible in a humble spirit, then the Word becomes meaningful for our handling of different problems. I'm always concerned that the biblical text is used and abused as a pretext for other purposes. This I cannot accept, though I realize that I, through the process of explanation, walk on the edge of a razor because I might also use, consciously or unconsciously, the text as a pretext. But this is the challenge to be religious at a moment of crisis, as is our time. Crisis need not be understood as a moment of decline, but following the original Greek meaning, as a moment of decision between two moments of great creativity. And that's what is influential in our interpretation of the biblical text. We live in a time of crisis; we have to listen to the Word and try to implement it in our life through interpretation. But again, I say, such interpretation might be open to wide efforts, as we have seen in many spiritual adventures in our days.

Contemporary Biblical Messages

P.S.: We've looked at the importance of the commandments and their relevance for today. We've talked about what it means to live according to the biblical mindset or mentality. Perhaps our readers would find it interesting if we simply took a number of contemporary issues and conversed about how we see the biblical message being implemented and applied to these very specific issues.

For example, sexual habits. From a Catholic point of view we start, as I indicated earlier, with the notion that sexuality is sacred, and it's a privileged moment of communication which requires the covenant of marriage. For us, as for the Hebrew prophets, marriage was a symbol of the relationship between God and His people. Saint Paul takes that image, and says it reflects the relationship between Christ and His Church. And therefore, for us the only appropriate environment for sexual activity is in the covenant of marriage. If one says that sex is good because it's created by God, and that it's sacred and it has a privileged moment in people's lives, then that automatically says that there are times in which it is inappropriate. So anything that is outside the bonds of marriage is beyond the pale, whether that's fornication or adultery or a rather contemporary issue — the sexual expression of love between two persons of the same sex.

L.K.: You referred to marriage and sexual ethics by emphasizing the concept of covenant in the Catholic concept of marriage. In our tradition, marriage is a contract that commits both parties to mutual respect and observance. The marriage liturgy talks about the obligation of each, the need to create a new entity rooted in the tradition of Judaism but open to a personal and community creativity. The seven blessings of the liturgy emphasize the need for that couple to build a new life in the meaning of our tradition. As a contract, this entity is also open to a break of the covenant by the act of divorce.

P.S.: While you correctly picked up on my use of the word "covenant" for marriage, I should note that in Catholic theology marriage is also considered a contract. It's interesting that under our previous Code of Canon Law from 1917, marriage was treated exclusively as a contract. And it's only in light of some of the insights of the biblical and patristic era and the post-conciliar period that we have begun to look upon marriage also as a covenant. The 1983 Code of Canon Law speaks of marriage in both senses. It would seem to me that in common practice when we are preparing couples for marriage, and certainly for the celebration of the liturgy, we tend to emphasize the covenantal aspect of it, and the contractual in a more legal or juridical context. These two are by no means exclusive of each other, but rather mutually reinforcing. You also hit immediately on a point of division between Catholics and Jews when you mentioned the question of divorce. For us the issue is treated by Jesus, Who obviously sided with a particular school of Jewish thought in banning all divorce, whereas other schools of thought accepted it for particular circumstances or under all circumstances.

L.K.: Yes, we believe in divorce in its two aspects, the Jewish theological aspect and also the legal or civil aspect. When a couple is seeking a divorce they go to the rabbinic tribunal, which listens to the case, considers the problems of the couple, and strongly recommends the possibility of reconciliation and rebuilding their marriage. When this is not possible the council gives a rabbinic divorce, which is expressed in a document that annuls the document of marriage, called *ketubah*. The *ketubah*, as I explained before, stresses the obligations of both husband and wife in their marriage experience. Personally, I have great reservations about the freedom of divorce. However, I feel there are times in the life of a couple that a divorce, because of a tragedy or serious problems, is necessary in order for both parties to rebuild their lives. But I'm still concerned about the wide popularity of divorce that diminishes for us the sanctity of the original marriage contract.

P.S.: This is also a source of great concern to us as Catholics. It's regrettable that Catholics in the United States divorce at approximately the same rate as non-Catholics. First of all, it means that our message has not gotten through clearly enough, and secondly, that American Catholics are probably more influenced by the secular society than they are by what should be their religious convictions. It would also be good to note, though, that the Catholic Church acknowledges the civil implications of divorce — namely, for purposes of child support, alimony or settlement of property. Where we draw the line is to say that while the divorce decree has civil effects it has no effect upon the essence of the marriage bond; and therefore, a Catholic would be permitted to get a divorce, but not to remarry.

L.K.: Once the rabbinic court gives a document of divorce, the couple can remarry. There is no further problem. But I feel it's sad, and my own pastoral experience about it has shown me that in many cases a divorce gives a man, especially, freedom to forget the past, and more especially, the care of his children. I have seen so many desperate women trying to rebuild their lives and the lives of their children because of the economic abandonment of the former husband. This matter should be taken into consideration very much by the judicial system in order to avoid irresponsibility.

Matters of Life and Death

P.S.: When people think of morality, most immediately begin to think about matters that we traditionally call life and death, and I think it would be interesting for our readers to have some idea of exactly where Catholics and Jews are, either in agreement or disagreement, on these very basic issues. Certainly, when we talk about life issues even people outside the Catholic Church immediately begin to think of the Church's stand on abortion, which is absolutely and unequivocally negative. I would be interested, Leon, in the range of opinion that exists within the Jewish community on that issue.

L.K.: It is very important to stress the matter of the "range of opinions" in the Jewish community. There is no unanimous stand on abortion. The Orthodox community is critical of abortion on demand, though the Conservatives and Reform followers would be more open to it. But even within the Orthodox community, there are different opinions about the need for abortion at a certain moment of life. The rabbinic tradition would point out that abortion is permitted in case of danger to the life of the mother; the fetus is considered part of the body of the mother. But as soon as a piece, a small piece, of the body of the baby is coming out of the mother's womb that child has an independent life. It is important to state that in cases of rape the rabbis would allow abortion. This was the case during the Second World War when the Nazi soldiers raped many Jewish women in occupied Europe. The rabbis would recommend abortion because the fetus was considered "an intruder," rather than part of the mother's life. I would say, however, that the general view is one of anguish concerning this very serious procedure, which is considered as something destructive to the body and spirit of the mother.

P.S.: When you mentioned the issue of the unborn child being considered an intruder, would that point of view be held by the Orthodox as well?

L.K.: I was referring to the opinion of Orthodox rabbis during the Second World War.

P.S.: Very often it's difficult for people in the Catholic community, as well as other Christians committed to the pro-life movement, to understand what looks like, at least on the surface, rather wholesale Jewish acceptance or even propagation of abortion, especially in light of Nazi techniques of declaring Jews non-persons and that same technique being operative in the United States regarding the life of the unborn. What insight would you have on that?

L.K.: I would never compare the Nazi genocide to abortion. I have many times criticized pro-life activists who have compared abortion to the Holocaust. The Holocaust was a planned ideological onslaught of the German Nazi structure, and abortion is not part of an apparatus that wants to destroy human life. I'm talking ideologically. I'm horrified, as are many Jews in the community, by abortion. But I also recognize that there are cases when there is no other way out but an abortion to avoid genetic problems or even emotional problems in the woman or in the couple. I will, however, like many of our Jewish spiritual leaders, declare that abortion is not a birth-control method. If it's used in that way, it is really an evil way of responding to birth and to a life situation.

A Variety of Views

P.S.: I think that would be a very consoling attitude if the position that you have just enunciated were more publicly known in the pro-life community. I have never heard it spoken by any Jews except some of the most Orthodox Jews who are themselves very involved in the pro-life movement.

You mentioned, Leon, abortion as a birth-control method, and certainly the statistics indicate that about 95 to 98 percent of the abortions performed in this country are used in precisely that manner. That brings us to the whole question of birth control and the Jewish attitude toward it. The Catholic position, which is reasonably well known, is that every act of human intercourse needs to be open to the propagation of life. And aside from natural methods of birth control — natural family planning, for example — the Catholic position is negative. Does that find any echo in Jewish theology, either historically or at present?

L.K.: Let us clarify the words. I cannot talk of a Jewish opinion, or a Jewish position on birth control. I have to talk about Jewish views on birth control reflecting the variety of religious opinions in the Jewish community. It was different up to a century or two ago, when Orthodoxy was the only form of religious Jewish life. Now, since modern times, the opinions are different. But I would also add that even in the Middle Ages there were different opinions among Orthodox thinkers. Again, I have to say that we don't have a magisterium, but rather different rabbinical and scholarly opinions on certain matters.

Specifically in relationship to birth control, the Orthodox attitude would be to recommend self-control instead of artificial ways of avoiding creation. The Conservative and Reform movements are more open to the use of birth control methods. There is also a whole section of our community which is not religiously committed who are in favor of birth control.

This is a delicate matter in Jewish life. It is ironic that some of our leaders are recommending birth control when our community suffered the death of six million Jews during the Second World War and our families do not grow as they did before. It is ironic that we as a people commanded by God have decided to lower our birth rate. But there is also a concern, even in our Orthodox community, about the welfare of the child and the family. For that reason, prudence in sexual life is recommended in order not to overcharge the family with economic problems. In our days especially, a family has to face hard decisions regarding everyday life, the education of children, charity, and all this should be taken into account in the formation of a family.

P.S.: The last paragraph resonates completely with the Catholic teaching on family planning, whether it was

Pope Pius XI or Pope Pius XII or Pope Paul VI in 1968 with his encyclical *Humanae Vitae*. All of the popes of the twentieth century have taken into account the fact that there is no moral necessity for Catholics to "increase and multiply" in an unrestricted manner but that the appropriate methods to use, as you speak of the Orthodox community, are self-control and self-restraint rather than the use of artificial methods.

Leon, you alluded to what some people would refer to as a "quality of life" ethic as a determining factor in whether or not new life should be brought into a family, and there would be broad agreement in the Catholic community on that issue. But that brings us to other bio-ethical concerns. What do you understand the "quality of life ethic" to include and to exclude? What are some possibilities, and what are some problems that you see there?

Maintaining Quality of Life

L.K.: By "quality of life" I refer to the possibilities of developing a creative spiritual and religious existence in the life of the individual, and very especially in the family. By quality of life I'm not talking about physical or economic advantages, but rather the possibility of living a religious life — a covenantal relationship — as an individual and a family. We are surrounded by so many social and economic pressures that many times we are not able to develop and perform our religious commitment. I dream of a society where there is freedom of religious action, but what I cannot accept is unrestrained freedom which justifies all sorts of adventures, both spiritually and socially. I'm very much concerned about that period of the '60s in the United States when we went through an inner transformation, rebelling against the Puritanism that is part of our American way. We went to extremes for which we are still paying a high price. On the other side, I'm also concerned by religious extremism, especially fundamentalism, whereby we deny basic freedoms to the individual in his search for a meaningful religious commitment.

P.S.: What you are describing in terms of quality of life has a very spiritual dimension to it, but I suspect that the average American who hears the expression understands a very different reality. For example, a whole new field on the horizon now is genetic engineering. As a result, parents are actually deciding the future of their child on the basis of how much intelligence they want the child to have, the hair color, the eye color — all of these variables which to them bespeak a "proper" quality of life. And even more astounding, that if they discover through various genetic tests that these qualities do not apparently exist in the unborn child, they simply do away with the child. At the other end of the life spectrum, deciding on the fate of one's grandmother on the basis of whether or not she has all of her mental capacities, or if she has physical difficulties which are either financially taxing or socially distressing. What would be your impressions of that type of approach to a quality of life ethic?

L.K.: My own consideration, and the consideration of many in the Jewish community, is that genetic engineering is like walking on a tight-rope. Sometimes we need genetic help to assist the couple who have difficulties conceiving a child, or with problems related to the human body in people who are facing certain diseases. Those are problems that genetic engineering can answer in a creative way and thus really advance life. But I am horrified by the possibility that a couple could decide that they are going to have a child with blue eyes or any other color, sex, etc. This is diabolical. It reminds us, especially Jews, of the experiments done by the Nazis in Auschwitz and other concentration camps. Men of science can be brilliant scholars but can also be the agents of the Devil in working on the human being. Again, I would ask for caution, but I wouldn't like to stop research.

In reference to the death of old people, I feel that we could follow a similar Nazi system. I abhor that. But I also recognize that some old people, after discussion with children and family, feel that they have come to an end of life because medical treatment is prolonging an agony rather than making life a meaningful, creative venture. Euthanasia, then, is open, as other fields of human enterprise — to walk on the edge of the razor. It could also call for fanaticism and the evil possibilities of the human mind.

P.S.: The Catholic attitude toward genetics, in general, is certainly positive. I think we have to make the point, for example, that the father of genetics was an Augustinian monk by the name of Gregor Mendel. Therefore, the Church is surely not opposed to scientific advances, and there are many wonderful things that can be done through the science of genetics. For instance, if one discovers that the child in the womb has a problem, by discovering it before birth it can sometimes be corrected, whereas if it is discovered five minutes after birth, it can never be dealt with. Thus that would be a tremendous help of genetics.

I think another question that we have to address in the religious community in general is the whole matter of whether or not technology must always be used. There are certain technologies which are available today which the human side of man should feel compelled to restrain. And simply because I can do something does not necessarily mean that I should or must do something. And then finally on the euthanasia question, what you have expressed would be by and large very acceptable in Catholic theology, which does not include the maintenance of life at all costs. But we would distinguish between an active and passive approach to this. Using extraordinary means to prolong human life may actually be either extremely painful, useless in the long run, or exorbitant to the point that another generation will be burdened for prolonging someone's life for a matter of a couple of weeks only. There's a big difference between deciding against that kind of treatment and giving Grandma a lethal injection, which is an active means to end life, rather than simply allowing human life to take its course.

L.K.: We recently had in our family a problem concerning life and death. My late mother-in-law was very ill, and she discussed with us the matter of ending her life. She was a very active person, involved in local political life, in cultural events, going to concerts, and suddenly she was unable to attend those activities. But it was not because of not being involved anymore that she thought about death, but about the quality of life. She felt that she was no longer a useful human being, an active, creative human being. She was just an object, and she couldn't stand that anymore. She died a natural death and her death was a very important, meaningful process for both Myra and myself. We shared life with my late mother-in-law, but we also shared her death. And this is an important event in the life of the family, to share death as well as life. Otherwise, death becomes a sort of taboo that nobody wants to talk about. We felt very lonely after Margie left, but we knew that we were at her side to the last moment. We shared even the moment when she was not able to talk. We shared the beauty of our family in that living experience.

In Judaism there is the custom to have services every evening to recite the *Kaddish*, the prayer for the deceased, in the company of friends and relatives. This is very meaningful because during those seven days we are able to work out the fact that person is not here physically anymore, but he or she is eternally at our side in a spiritual presence.

Learning from Life and Death

P.S.: As you were describing the situation of your mother-in-law's death, Leon, it seemed to me that one of the important things that religious people can and should do for another is to help someone die, and to bring the person to a deeper realization of the meaning of human life. For instance, one helps the dying person revise his or her understanding of the meaning of life; thus your mother-in-law, for example, who was a woman extremely active in cultural and political events, would be brought to understand that she was reaching a different plateau in human existence at that point. And that is certainly a very important and loving task for family members and religious and pastoral workers to engage in. It also reminds me, for instance, of a similar need when parents discover that they have just given birth to a deformed child. I have seen innumerable situations in which that child, who in terms of very crude standards of a quality of life ethic, had nothing to offer, could never even know his name, perhaps. And yet that child has become the source of creativity and love within a family that under many other circumstances could have been a very self-centered, materialistic gathering of people. But the child, in essence, or an older person or anyone who is disabled, as a matter of fact, can be a source for bringing out the best in people.

L.K.: Let me add a personal dimension to what we are talking about. The death of my mother-in-law helped me work out the death of my daughter Myriam Gabriela, who died in a car accident years ago. As I said earlier, I was in the car and was unconscious for two weeks in the hospital. When I woke up I tried to relive the accident and I couldn't; I still cannot remember what happened. And I went through the experience of grieving after the family had grieved already for a week after the accident. This created innumerable problems in the family. But the death of my mother-in-law helped me in many ways to relive that time of grieving and to be at peace with the people who died and passed away. And I use the words "passed away" physically, because spiritually both Margie and Myriam are always at our side. Both my wife and I feel that death, and life as well, are divine experiences that require our understanding and working out. They are not end processes; they are the beginning of new dimensions of life that require our attention and reflection.

Exploring Family Values

P.S.: What you have described, Leon, in terms of the death of your mother-in-law assisting you in understanding and coming to grips with the death of your daughter I believe points out what we mean about the connectedness of all reality — the chain of life, if you will. And we are surely here to assist each other in coming to grips with the very important issues of life and death. In our discussions of life issues another word pops up consistently, and that's the word "family." And in the past ten years, at least, there's been a great concern expressed in society-at-large about the decline of so-called "family values." What do you, as a Jew, understand family values to mean and to be?

L.K.: I confess, Peter, that the expression "family values" makes me feel very uneasy. It is because of my own historical and political experiences in the past. I remember that in my native Argentina those who defended family values were generally Fascists, many of them torturers and the state police, or certain Catholic leadership that, despite Vatican II, still lived in the Middle Ages. And not in the best part of the Middle Ages. By that expression I stress the unity of the family, the solidarity of the family, the close relationship of friends with children, the idea of an extended family despite geographical distance, and a need to continue the idea of family through memory and mutual action.

Our tradition says in Passover, "*zahor*" — remember. This is the goodness of family life, to remember the past, but not to have that past imposed upon us as a methodology. The goodness of family life is to project a unity, a solidarity for each other, and at the same time continuing the tradition of centuries, making it meaningful for our days. That also means that children have the power to create, in addition to the creativity by their parents. In that way, the family becomes like a small Israel, a covenantal God-peoplehood relationship fostering and implementing the values of our tradition. But I don't want to make out of family values a political ideology. Sometimes it reminds me of that character of the French writer Honoré de Balzac, who is a politician defending family values and motherhood, while at the same having several lovers.

P.S.: Everything that you have said I would underscore and write even larger for the Catholic perspective.

L.K.: Peter, sometimes we have to disagree with each other. Otherwise, it's going to be boring for our readers.

Ships in the Night

P.S.: When you refer to the Jewish family as a "little Israel," it reminds me of the Second Vatican Council insight into the family as an "*ecclesiola*," that is, a little church or a domestic church. The Fathers of the Church and the great spiritual writers in the Catholic tradition, most especially Pope John Paul II, have emphasized over and over again that the primary source for religious and moral values for Catholics is found in the context of the Christian family. Nor should it come as a surprise to us to discover that many of the "traditional values" or family values have not been communicated to at least one if not two generations precisely at the moment when family life has broken down dramatically.

When I was teaching at a major Catholic university, I was shocked when a boy told me that even though he was living at home with his mother, father, brothers and sisters, he had not seen his father for nine days. The boy had slept at home every night, as had his father, but their schedules were in conflict because of work and school and there was no such thing as a family meal anymore; in point of fact, these two men were ships in the night at a very critical time in the formation of the life of this young Catholic gentleman.

L.K.: There is also an American reality in relation to family values. In the United States seldom does a whole family live together in the same city. The reality is that, as in my own case, my daughter went to study at a college three hours from New York and now lives in Brooklyn and my son went to study in Indiana and now lives in New Mexico. And it becomes difficult to get together even once a year. This was not the reality in my native Argentina, where my parents lived in the same house for thirty years, and they moved to an apartment because they just couldn't live anymore in a big house because of their age. What is important is a sense of unity. Thank God, the phone helps to relate to children in far-away places. But presence is still very important.

P.S.: It seems to me that we can't simply transfer the family situation of a generation ago, let alone a century ago, into the contemporary context. That may work for some very self-contained groups like the Amish or even certain segments of the more Orthodox branches of Judaism. But, in truth, those of us who have confronted modernity have to do so in a creative way, so that we take the basic values and present them in a contemporary key, as you say, taking cognizance of distances and ways to transmit a heritage under admittedly difficult circumstances. When we consider the whole issue of transmitting family values, one of the biggest difficulties that religious families have is the role of the media. Whether that is the rock music that blares out at children's ears, or the hard-core or soft-core pornography — all of these become serious problems for parents who at one level want to protect their children from this, and yet at the same time realize that they have to prepare their children to deal with this phenomenon in their own right.

L.K.: There is another reality that many of us are facing. It is a question of cultural and social differences. In my case, my parents were immigrants from Poland to Argentina and they had to learn a new language; they now speak nearly perfect Spanish, but they were not born in Argentina. I was born there. I was educated there until university, and then I came to the United States to study, and I remember that in my youth both my brother and I lived double lives. One was the life of the family, where Yiddish was the everyday language, where customs and traditions from Jewish Poland were a reality in our daily life; at the same time, my brother and I lived the life of young people under a dictatorship, fighting Fascism and reading books that my father never dreamed that his children were reading. Let me give you one example.

When I was thirteen, one "pornographic" novel that was going around in high school was *Nana*, by Émile Zola. This book, when compared with the literary junk that we are faced with today, is very innocent, but thirty or forty years ago it was the novel read by anxious adolescents. I read it at home, hiding it from my father, and finally he caught me. He asked me what it was, so I said to him that I was reading a novel about a poor girl who tried to lead a decent life, married, had children, created a family, etc. I really rewrote *Nana* for my father. My father told me that I shouldn't read novels because novels are a waste of time, and are also "diabolical" objects. He made a pun between the Yiddish words for "diabolic" and "novel."

Thirty or forty years ago, when I went back to Argentina as a rabbi, my father told me with a very special smile that he was reading a novel in Yiddish. It was *Nana* by Émile Zola. I pointed out to him that there are more interesting novels, but my father said, "You should be ashamed. You read this book, the life of a lost woman, when you were a kid. What other books were you reading when you were a child?" I didn't answer my father, but I realized that between his generation, his experience and mine, there was a gap very difficult to reach.

At the same time, I remember once discussing French literature with my own son, and I told him about André Gide, the French writer who wrote a book about a homosexual in the 1900s. Daniel read the book and said, "But, Father, why didn't he come out of the closet?" Daniel didn't realize that this book would pretty soon be perhaps one hundred years old, and it was a different world. He was expressing an American dimension that didn't exist in my own life in far-away Argentina.

Should We Censor?

P.S.: I guess the question that we have to ask is: How far can or should parents and religious leaders — well, let's be honest and use the word we're really looking for — censor the materials to be read by their children? And then taking it a step further, what about government censorship of certain materials being harmful, particularly to the good of children?

L.K.: Again, Peter, I'm trembling. When it comes to censorship, the word brings back immediately my old youthful experience of living under a dictatorship. There was censorship; it was not possible to talk about politics, to read certain books, and only through smuggling were we able to get books that were essentially innocent but were considered a danger to the dictatorship. I feel that there should be in family life a certain amount of censorship. The young child shouldn't read certain books, because it doesn't help his or her education and will hurt him eventually. Now, I don't want to exercise censorship as an authoritarian tool. I feel that censorship is necessary for the development of the young person, who eventually would be able to read freely what he wants. Regarding government censorship, I confess my great uneasiness. I would like the government to have a greater censorship of what's going on in places where pornography is sold. It is horrible. It denigrates human life, it denigrates women in a terrible way, and I'm surprised that the feminist movement hasn't been "burning" those businesses where they sell pornography. But what I feel is important for the parents is to talk about sexuality to their children at the appropriate time. This is what we did with our children. Otherwise, it becomes a mystery that they try to uncover and so get into all sorts of adventures. For me, family life involves censorship at times, information all the time, and an ongoing dialogue with the children, even if they cannot understand or do not want to accept our ideas. Let me give you one example that comes to my mind.

I remember when my children were younger, we would celebrate Friday night dinner at home — the *Shabbat* — and I wouldn't allow the children to leave the house afterwards. The high school of my daughter used to offer a dance every Friday evening, and Ruthie was not allowed to go. I cannot describe her humor at dinnertime. The

Shabbat celebration was always darkened by her attitude. But my position was very clear. *Shabbat* is a sacred family celebration, it's a time that we are together, in the presence of God, celebrating our covenantal relationship, and the whole family has to be together enjoying that special time in the week after so much work by the parents and the children in their schools. It is ironic that twenty-five years later Ruthie thanked me with a big smile and a kiss for the fact that I didn't let her go to the dances on Friday nights. She told me, "I learned a lesson of spiritual commitment that I will transmit to my children."

P.S.: I think that people with a religious conviction have to train their children to be different. The psychology behind this is very, very strong in the Catholic community. It was much stronger when I was a boy. For instance, I think of going to the boardwalk with my father on a Friday night and smelling Italian sausages and peppers being made and sold, and saying to him that I wanted one. At which point he would always remind me that it was Friday, a day of abstinence from meat, and that Catholics take that law seriously. Rather humorously, I remember one day he struck a deal with me that if I "behaved myself" he would remain at the boardwalk with me until one minute after midnight and would treat me to a sausage sandwich. Thirty years later, I smile at that somewhat naive approach to reality, but nonetheless he reinforced for me the importance of being different and retaining one's religious commitment in an environment which did not foster that commitment. Similarly, I remember wanting to go see a film called *The Cardinal*, and again, like you, Leon, I look back at that film and realize that it is very mild compared to anything that's available today. But in fact, that film had a condemned rating from the National Catholic Legion of Decency. It was first of all condemned because the priest's sister was involved in fornication and perhaps adultery. Secondly, she got herself involved with an unwanted pregnancy and there was serious talk about an abortion. And thirdly, the man himself took a leave of absence from the priesthood twenty years before that was "fashionable." For all those reasons, the film was condemned. I add now, I think rightly so. However, I wanted to see the film and I told my father I wanted to see it. He thought about it and came back to me and said, "We will go see it together, and you may view it on condition that when the film is over, we will have a two-hour discussion about the issues that were raised in the film." I was ten years old. When my father mentioned it to the parish priest later, he agreed that he thought it was "a good idea for Peter to have seen the film, especially since he wants to be a priest." The priest then asked me not to let other students know that I had seen the film.

But I think that's the kind of "censorship" that makes sense. First of all, it starts with the premise that we are different. As Christians we are reminded of the fact that Jesus encourages us to be the leaven in society and the salt of the earth; in order to be either of those things, one has to be comfortable with his religious heritage and the difference that makes between his life and the life of the "outsider."

L.K.: Peter, I'm very happy for a word that you used. You said "a religious person is a different person." I have been saying that about being Jewish. I point out that to be Jewish is to be different and I sometimes get nasty looks or even nastier comments. When I was young in Argentina a professor of mine in high school, a known Fascist, used to say, "Jews are different. Why are they different? Why can't they be like us?" He wouldn't say Catholics, he would say human beings. But what I stress is that to be religious, to be in a covenantal relationship with God, makes me a different person, not better or worse than other persons, but a different person, with a commitment of action and projecting covenantal values in my life. This is what I have taught my children, and I can see now that, despite their youthful rebellion, they affirm what I used to say twenty or twenty-five years ago. But now it's part of them, though it was transmitted by me or my parents. That is, that to be religious is to be different.

Chapter Six

The Blessings of Pluralism

The Necessary Separation

P.S.: When we consider differences, that logically leads us to consider the question of pluralism. What is the relationship between one's individual convictions and those of another person? How do people of varying, and sometimes very strongly differing, convictions relate to each other in a "pluralistic society"? Sometimes in history people haven't done this all too well. At other moments, it seems to have been "pulled off" a little bit better. In the United States, with the conviction that "separation of Church and State" is a reality, some people have come to the position that religious values need to be excluded from the public forum. Others see or hold that religious values are such a source of tension that they should not be discussed outside either the home or the religious institution. And yet others would look at the present moment as needing a fresh infusion of religious values, sometimes done subtly, sometimes done through the democratic process, and at other times just very forcefully negotiated. The Catholic community looks upon the constitutional idea of separation of Church and State with favor but a degree of suspicion, for the simple reason that often enough that constitutional principle is used in a way as to exclude religion from civic and public reality.

L.K.: For us Jews, pluralism is a blessing. We have lived through the European alienation for centuries, and the possibility of exercising your religious commitment in freedom and with the respectful acceptance of others is a blessing. Pluralism can take very extreme points, as you just remarked, in the name of pluralism and total separation of Church and State. We are very eager not to have religion and religious organizations involved in the political and social life of the country. But this is also open to dangers. I feel very uneasy about prayer in public schools. I feel that prayer reflects the covenantal relationship of Jews and Christians and other religious groups and should be expressed in that way. But if a teacher prepares a prayer that is so general and doesn't refer to any specific aspect of God according to our traditions, the prayer is just a collection of nouns and adjectives with no real meaning at all. I feel that this is a mockery rather than religious life. I also . . .

P.S.: If I might interject a point here, it would be a rather standard conviction in the Catholic community that prayer in public schools is not an incredibly desirable reality. I would hold very strongly that the Constitution, properly understood, does not outlaw a generic prayer in public schools. I think it a revisionist approach to constitutional law to suggest that the Constitution does forbid this. That having been said, though, I know from personal experience that prayer can be used in many ways in a government school setting which does no justice to prayer or to the individual. For example, when my father's family moved to New Jersey from Massachusetts, there was no space in the Catholic school for him, and he was on a waiting list for the remainder of the year. He was forced to pray the "Protestant version" of the Our Father, or Lord's Prayer. Because he refused to do that, he was kept back in the fourth grade. Certainly that approach to prayer is very, very poor. Secondly, I'm opposed to prayer in government schools, especially today, because of the problems that exist in these schools. I do not want a prayer to keep parents from realizing some of the very deep problems that exist in those schools; I'm uncomfortable with a prayer being used to give a religious aura to other aspects of school life which my religious convictions abhor. But in this instance, the position of the Catholic community would diverge seriously from several Protestant groups, particularly of a more fundamentalist Christian bent, who have no problem whatsoever in suggesting that the basic problems of American public education began precisely when prayer was removed from the government schools.

L.K.: For us Jews, the question of prayer in public schools brings back memories of past experiences. My parents in Poland, and I in Argentina — two overwhelmingly Catholic countries — had to go through experiences of imposed prayers in high school. I remember that when I studied in Buenos Aires we had to listen to the prayer of a teacher that was essentially a Catholic prayer, and Jews and Protestants were silent in class. We had to take courses in morality, essentially Catholic morality, while the rest of the students were taking catechism. There was an arrangement between General Peron and the Catholic leadership in Argentina. This political alliance hurt not only the religious minorities, but in the long run the Church itself. Essentially, I feel that any religious presence, in prayer or any form of liturgy, hurts the religiosity of the students and hurts the religious freedom of our country.

P.S.: As a professional educator, as well as a priest, I have very strong convictions about the inseparability of religion from the process of one's general education. I do not believe that a government school system should be used to inculcate a sectarian point of view, which is why we Catholics have always argued in the United States for pluralism, not only in society but in educational forms. I don't think it's possible to educate a child in a holistic manner by excluding the religious element. And therefore, Catholics have pressed for a plurality or variety of educational systems which would reflect parental values; the task of government in that instance would not be to run a school system, but simply to provide the wherewithal such that parents could choose the most appropriate educational environment for their children. I know there's a great deal of division within the Jewish community on that issue. And, once again, like so many other matters there is a wide spectrum of opinion. Perhaps you could share some of that with us.

The Role of Government

L.K.: One concern of the Jewish community is the matter of federal aid to parochial schools. In general, it is felt that, though many Jews are for it, federal aid to non-public schools will foster differences and also prejudice. One has to remember that we have different memories of parochial schools from our own youth in Argentina or in Europe. In those countries, parochial schools got help from the state and were centers of anti-Semitism and extremism. This was my experience in the past, though it might have changed somewhat in Argentina in the last years. I doubt that it has changed in Poland, where the anti-Jewish feeling is still a reality, despite the fact that there are practically no Jews in that country. But I do feel that we need, in the context of American pluralism and democracy, to rethink the question of help to non-public schools, especially since those non-public schools are excellent tools of education in our major cities.

P.S.: You made several points, Leon, which I think would be healthy to engage. First you used the expression, "federal aid to parochial schools," which, I grant you, is a rather common expression but one which I shy away from at all costs for any number of reasons. First of all, as a Catholic educator and priest, I do not want one penny of government money to go into a Catholic school for the simple reason that "he who pays the piper calls the tune." On the contrary, Catholics argue for a system of vouchers or tax credits which enables money to flow to parents regardless of their religious affiliation or conviction. Such a method also has the advantage of making a philosophical statement at the same time — namely, that parents are the primary educators of their children and the money goes to parents, who then decide where they want their child educated, so that the parent is the conduit of the funding. It also eliminates all of the constitutional questions which are raised about the separation of Church and State. Secondly, you make the point that there is a concern among some Jews that parochial schools foster prejudice. It's important to understand that at least as far as Catholic parochial schools are concerned the most ecumenical, open-minded Catholics who exist are those who are products of Catholic schools. I think if we reflect on this carefully we'll understand why that's the case. If a child is carefully formed in his own religious tradition and very comfortable with who he is in his own community, and then with his position vis-à-vis the community-at-large, he can be extremely open in dealing with other people. He's unthreatened by the differences and in fact sees the differences as healthy rather than problematic. All the surveys that have been done on Catholic school graduates show, contrary to your fears, that Catholic children who have attended Catholic school have a much higher rate of openness, particularly to Jews, than Catholic children who have gone to public school. The last point that I would make is that I find it at least a little strange that so many American Jews, particularly of a more liberal bent, are opposed to government aid to parochial school children when, in point of fact, in Israel the government does aid all schools, including the Catholic schools.

L.K.: At times when I listen to criticism about federal aid to parochial schools among people of different religious convictions, I feel that it reflects essentially a sort of anti-Catholicism. This prejudice is present in our days in films or books and is becoming part of a national folklore. I'm concerned about it, because Catholics in the United States are sometimes more advanced in their thought in social matters and spiritual matters than their fellow citizens of different religious commitments. At times, talking to Catholic friends, I feel that I am a "reactionary" and they are the liberals, though they vote for conservative causes. But anti-Catholicism is a reality in American life. It was manifest in the days of the Kennedy political campaign, when the future president was accused of working for Rome rather than Washington. That kind of political reactionary thought has stopped, but it was present in the campaign of 1960.

Living the Differences

P.S.: One of the projects that you and I collaborated on many years ago, Leon, was during the time when I worked for the Catholic League for Religious and Civil Rights. A terrible play had made its debut on Broadway called *Sister Mary Ignatius Explains It All for You.* It was a source of great comfort to Catholics that Jews at an official and public level would make common cause with us in protesting a vicious attack on Catholicism in general and the parochial school system and women religious in particular. The question of anti-Catholicism is something that definitely needs to be studied from an historical and sociological perspective, and perhaps also from a psychological point of view. But what I would like to underscore today is that, very often, people who attack Catholicism do so in very subtle ways, generally not by attacking Catholic doctrinal matters, like the virginity of Mary or the presence of Christ in the Eucharist; rather it is our moral positions which are attacked. At root they are saying that Catholicism is "okay" as long as Catholics keep their mouths shut and don't act or sound "too Catholic." As a Jew, you can understand very well what that means. Jews are acceptable as long as they don't look or act like Jews in American society. And that is pandemic to American culture. I think that, as Arthur Schlesinger put it, anti-Catholicism is the dirty little secret of American history and not far behind anti-Catholicism is anti-Semitism in American society as well. Someone has even referred to anti-Catholicism as the anti-Semitism of the left. It's certainly easier for a Reform Jew to pass for a mainstream American than it is for a committed Catholic or an Orthodox Jew. Hence, to the extent that we don't act out our religious convictions, we're acceptable. And I think that's why the media love to highlight "renegade Catholics," because it demonstrates that they have no problem with these people and therefore it's the more "radical" type of observance of Catholicism that's difficult.

L.K.: I would like to stress and share with the community-at-large that we religious people, both Jewish and Christian, are different and need the freedom of exercising our difference in our society. But I'd also like to say that it's not only to *proclaim* difference; the crucial matter is to *live* that difference in our society.

Fighting Racism in Society

P.S.: While we acknowledge our differences, readers will see rather starkly that the moral convictions of religious Jews and Christians are unbelievably similar, and indeed there's a great convergence. It seems to me that one of the important fall-outs of this realization is that there are certain issues on which we can work together very creatively. And one of those would seem to be the whole problem of racism and its renewal in great force in American society.

L.K.: I would like to dialogue on racism, as well as anti-Semitism. At times I feel that racism is the "original sin" of the United States, and I apologize for the use of a theological term that belongs to your commitment but not necessarily to mine. The way we treated the black community and the Indian community in the United States requires our reckoning of the past as well as our relationship with these minorities in the future. Anti-black feelings have been in the conscious and the unconscious of American society for a long time and require our total attention. It is a sin, and John Paul II said a few months ago in Rome that anti-Semitism is a sin — to consider another person lower than ourselves because of color, different religion or beliefs. It is an arrogance of the heart that took humanity to the horror of the concentration camps or Stalin's diabolical Gulag. But it is our obligation, especially in a pluralistic society, to denounce racism and to teach our children and congregants the need to accept the other, by difference of belief or color, as a person of God. Otherwise, we make out of that person an object of contempt. And I'm not talking of an ideal plan of acceptance. I'm referring to the practical aspect of accepting the other as a human being, of accepting the other as a person of God.

P.S.: I think one of the mistakes that was made in the '60s was twofold. First, the conviction that racism could be confronted simply on the basis of legislation. The 1964 Civil Rights Act was good and needed, but many people then came to the conclusion that racism had now been overcome in American society. In reality, however, that thought enabled racism to live underground for a very, very long period of time. In a related context, I frequently remind pro-life activists that if they think that enacting anti-abortion legislation will eliminate abortion, they are very foolish and naive. I am completely in favor of every law to restrict abortion as much as possible, but I am not silly enough to imagine that will eliminate the problem of abortion. Similarly with racism. Merely having laws on the books, and even enforcing laws on the books, does not necessarily change men's hearts. The second concern that I have about our approach to racism is that very often we tend to look upon people who are different, whether that is racially or religiously or ethnically, as people whose differences we "tolerate." Tolerance is a very American concept. But to me tolerance is a negative notion, not a positive one. What we need to stress is appreciation for the differences. The French proverb, *"Vive la différence,"* is exactly what will destroy racism and every other kind of "ism" which strikes at the heart of the human person.

L.K.: Excellent, Peter, excellent. I have to tell you that I dislike the word "tolerance" thoroughly. I don't want to be tolerated by anybody; I want to be accepted as a human being, with my commitment and my difference. And that relates to racism. I do not tolerate a black person or an Indian; I accept him or not, based on political difference or ideological differences. But essentially, I accept him as a human being; I don't tolerate. We can tolerate only medicines or antibiotics, but in everyday life we have to accept the other as a person of God.

A Working Dialogue

P.S.: In what areas, Leon, can the Catholic and Jewish communities work together to deal with the general problem of racism? I think we can get more specific about anti-Semitism or anti-Catholicism at another stage, but just in the generic area of racism.

L.K.: By direct dialogue. By this I mean to establish an on-going conversation with black leadership of all different commitments in order to clarify situations and to achieve what I call "peace." Peace is not the opposite of war in Hebrew, but it is the completion of the creative process. I am concerned that there is extremism both in the white community and in the black community. I hear of black leadership who believe that violence or living by themselves — creating a second republic within our republic — is a solution to racism. It is not. What is important is that we should relate to each other: to talk, to discuss the differences, always having in mind the common good and the fact that we want to live in a democratic society that is an example to the world.

An image haunts my inner life — that of a recent TV program in which a black soldier who liberated a concentration camp returned to his city in the southern part of the United States. He went to a store to buy an ice cream and there was a group of German war prisoners who were served first because they were white. He was served last because he was black. Here was a liberator of a concentration camp who saw what these officials, or their fellow soldiers in Germany, might have done, and despite that the owner of the store served those murderers first. This image is ever-present in my imagination concerning the lack of respect for the human being in the exercise of racism.

P.S.: When we move from prejudice against race to prejudice against religion, many of the same principles apply. And it's important to admit that such prejudice exists. Certainly there are Catholics who were trained, probably not officially, but through the culture to have an anti-Semitic bias. I think the majority of that prejudice has been eradicated in the Catholic community in the United States over the past twenty years. As I mentioned at the very beginning of our conversations I never knew that kind of prejudice as a child myself. But where it does still exist it surely needs to be addressed through our Catholic school system, through the preaching and teaching of clergy, etc. On the other hand, there is in my experience a very strong strain of anti-Catholicism in various segments of the Jewish community. I think Catholic readers might be interested to know (a) is that being addressed, and (b) if so, in what ways?

L.K.: I feel that there is a lack of knowledge in our community-at-large about Christianity. We know what Christianity has done to the Jewish people through the centuries, especially in Europe. But the essentials of the Christian faith are unknown. For that reason, I devoted the first issue of the Anti-Defamation League's newest publication, *In Dialogue*, to Christianity. Father Michael Carroll, of the Archdiocese of Philadelphia, prepared a basic study on the main ideas of Christianity, both spiritual and theological, for the formation of Jewish readers. I feel in that way this short study will help Jews who want to participate in the interfaith dialogue by providing them with all the basics of the faith of the other person. The issues follow my own study, "Towards a Jewish Understanding of Christianity." Mind you the language, Peter. I don't know if twenty years ago I would have written such an article. It took me much time, much conversation, studying Christianity and realizing that the interfaith dialogue is a dual process. Christians have to overcome prejudice, and we have to overcome memories of the past. In a pluralistic society, where there is respect for each other, whatever happened in Latin America or in Europe doesn't have any relationship to the present experience. If we insist on a connection then we believe in a Marxist way in the repetition of history. It's something that not even the Marxists think anymore.

P.S.: When we reflect on prejudices of any kind, that leads us to one of the biggest problems that humanity faces in every century: What do we mean by "peace," and what is the rationale, if there could be, for war? You alluded to a definition or an understanding of peace which reminds me of the Second Vatican Council's "*Gaudium et Spes,*" the Pastoral Constitution on the Church in the Modern World. In that document, the Council Fathers make the point that peace is not "the mere absence of war." I think that the definition of peace as the mere absence of war is a very impoverished notion. It puts the lie to the biblical notion of peace as wholeness and harmony and unity. But we also know that peace cannot exist if we do not have peaceable people. And where there are tensions and unresolved difficulties between and among individuals or groups of individuals, the destruction of peace through war is a logical and real possibility. And so, I guess it would be important to ask ourselves to think about when war is justified from a Jewish and Catholic perspective.

L.K.: Jewish participation in war is a new phenomenon for us. I want to remind you that, up to the nineteenth century, Jews were not allowed to get into the armies of European nations of feudal lords, and it was only after the French Revolution, especially in the nineteenth century, that Jews participated in wars in different countries. The idea of the legality and the need of war became meaningful after the creation of the State of Israel. Israel was born out of a war with neighboring countries, a war that has been repeated as a devastating experience through the years. Jews in general would consider war as a necessary evil to preserve life or to protect the community.

This is evident in the different war experiences of the State of Israel throughout her existence. It was a special reality in the Second World War, when we were the victims all over Europe, and were not able to fight back because we didn't belong to any army. In the uprising of the Warsaw Ghetto fifty years ago, the Jewish fighters didn't start a real war against the Nazis, but it was only a proclamation of the right to be Jewish in the midst of such an awful persecution. War is considered a horrible event, but a necessary matter when it relates to the defense of human life and the life of the community.

P.S.: Catholic theology attaches primary importance to human life and the preservation of human life, but we also believe that there are certain values that are so critically important that it is not only possible but even meritorious to sacrifice one's life for those values. In the Early Church, at a time when Christianity was a despised religion, the question of a Christian serving in the military gave rise to a kind of pacifism which was not the normal situation, but would develop into the normative situation for centuries to come. The Christian's holding back from war was also related to the question of idolatry in the pagan state of Rome, since fighting under the Roman banner constituted, in effect, accepting the entire pagan religious system. Therefore, I think it's rather incorrect when some theological revisionists in Christianity today suggest that Christianity at its roots was pacifist. On the contrary, Christianity would have the Hebrew notion, standard from the times of the patriarchs and the prophets and the kings, that war was indeed something which was, as you put it, a necessary evil under certain circumstances. With Christianity moving out of the catacombs, the theology and philosophy related to war needed some precision, and that came into focus especially through the work of Saint Augustine, who enunciated for the first time, in very clear fashion, what has come to be known as the "just war theory." Interestingly enough, we saw this just war theory applied, perhaps for the first time in the modern era, by a government rather than by the Church, in the Gulf War. President Bush was at great pains to demonstrate that all of the conditions of the just war theory had been verified before moving America into the sphere of war. Those conditions, very briefly, are that the belligerent action must be a last resort; the war must be called by a legitimate authority; the war must always be a defensive action; the means used must be proportionate to the attack and the danger that has been leveled by the aggressor; and, finally, that civilian populations must never be the target of such activity.

L.K.: The theological consideration of war is open to different attitudes from our faith commitment. As I said before, war is a recent experience in Jewish life. Before the creation of the State of Israel we were the victims of war experiences, but we were not very often involved in wars as soldiers. The exception was, perhaps, in Germany in the First World War, or in France, or in American wars. In the rest of the world we haven't played any significant role. In the specific case of Argentina there had been practically no Jews following military careers. On the contrary, no Jews have, to my knowledge, attended the military school. There might have been an exception, perhaps somebody who converted, but Jews were not involved in anything related to the military. War is a new experience for us. The theological understanding of war is also a new matter of discourse in our community.

And this is taking us to a consideration of theological conversation. Our kind of conversation is a special American phenomenon, that eventually will influence the world beyond. It is not common to have this kind of conversation, publicly or in books, in other countries. This opens the possibility, not only of talking to each other, but also to consider dialogue in a theological manner. There are critics in my own community who are very suspicious of theological conversation, and recently one of them said that, "Dialogue is acceptable as long as matters of theology are taboo." I find this a rather peculiar statement. When we talk as religious people, we talk theologically. Whenever I consider any matters, as we did before — war and peace, death or divorce — I do it from my theological sources, and I do not use sociology or philosophy. Essentially, we talk theology.

A Catholic-Jewish Dialogue — With Theology

P.S.: What the rabbi in question is arguing for seems to feed into the secularism of the moment in our society. I'm sure that is not his intention. But if genuine, intelligent human discourse must be sanitized of religion then in fact he would perhaps be rather more comfortable on the board of directors of the American Civil Liberties Union than as an Orthodox rabbi.

L.K.: Excellent, and no further comment. I feel that the theological consideration in our dialogue will grow as time passes. It is critical in order to understand our commitments and our interchange.

The goodness of pluralism — of democracy — is the fact that we can talk about or any   subject from our own religious points of view, respectful of the other as a person of God.

P.S.: I think it important to note and to highlight that the only reason that you and I are having this dialogue is precisely because of our religious convictions. There would be no other reason in the world to get us together to discuss matters of great importance, and if that is the case, then it makes no sense to say that having come together, we must keep theology at bay, when, in point of fact, that is the glue that will hold our individual relationship together as well as any potential relationship between our communities.

L.K.: Our tradition points out that when two or three persons are together talking about religious life, the presence of God is among them. That's what I feel in our conversation. It's the presence of God in our midst, though we might have different understandings of that presence in our personal religious life or the life of our community. But God is present, and this allows us to face the many problems in our society or in our inner lives, having that chain in common: that the two of us are people of God, committed religiously, and willing to share that presence of God without trying to proselytize the other.

Glossary

Catholic Terms

Advent: The four-week period which inaugurates the Church year and prepares for Christmas; it is marked by a spirit of anxious but joyful anticipation of the three comings of Christ: as the Babe of Bethlehem; in the sacraments; as Judge at the end of time.

Baptism: The first sacrament received by a believer (as an infant if belonging to a Christian family or as an adult if a convert) in which a person, through the pouring of water and the gift of the Holy Spirit, has the inherited sin of Adam and Eve removed from the soul and is incorporated into the Church.

Catechesis: The process by which believers are introduced to the Catholic Faith and then nourished in the Faith; therefore, while it begins in childhood, it is in fact a life-long process of education. The person responsible for this type of Christian formation is commonly called a catechist, while the book of instruction is often termed a catechism.

Code of Canon Law: The body of laws governing Catholic life for the Latin or Roman Rite, most recently updated in 1983. The Code does not usually treat matters related to liturgy, but it does concern most other rights and duties of all in the Church — laity, religious, and clergy alike. A separate code exists for Catholics who belong to the Eastern rites.

Confirmation: The sacrament which seals the Sacrament of Baptism through the imposition of hands and anointing with sacred chrism, a mixture of olive oil and balm.

Eucharist: The sacrament of the Body and Blood of Christ, left to the Church by Jesus during the Last Supper on Holy Thursday, the night before He died. That meal is generally thought to have been a Passover supper.

Holy Orders: This sacrament consists of three ministries: those of deacon, priest and bishop. It is conferred on a man by a bishop and establishes what is called a permanent character (that is, one cannot cease to be a minister of the Church although one can be permitted to lay aside the exercise of the ministry for certain reasons). Deacons may baptize solemnly, preach and distribute Holy Communion; priests are empowered to celebrate the Eucharist, absolve from sin and anoint the sick; bishops, possessing "the fullness of the priesthood," may perform all the functions of the lower clergy and also ordain other men.

Host: This word comes from the Latin *hostia*, meaning "victim"; it refers to the unleavened wafer used in the celebration of the Eucharist and received as Holy Communion. It got this name since Christ is the "victim" in the offering of the Eucharistic Sacrifice.

Lauds: Morning prayer.

Lectionary: The liturgical book in which are arranged the Scriptures assigned to be read at Mass for every day of the year and for the celebration of the various sacramental rites.

Lent: The forty-day period of penance, beginning on Ash Wednesday, in preparation for the solemn celebration of Christ's resurrection from the dead on Easter Sunday.

Liturgy: The official public worship of the Church, which would include the celebration of Mass and all seven sacraments (Baptism, Confirmation, Holy Eucharist, Penance, Matrimony, Holy Orders, Sacrament of the Sick), which are the rites established by Christ to impart divine grace or to deepen the life of God in the soul of a believer.

Liturgy of the Eucharist: The second half of the Mass during which the gifts of bread and wine are presented, transformed into the Body and Blood of Christ through the ministry of the priest and the work of the Holy Spirit, and then received as spiritual food in Holy Communion.

Liturgy of the Word: The first half of the Mass which contains the proclamation of the Sacred Scriptures and the sermon or homily, commenting on the assigned texts and relating them to the daily life of the liturgical assembly.

Magisterium: The teaching authority of the Catholic Church, consisting of the Pope and the bishops teaching in union with him, established by Jesus Christ to safeguard the integrity of Catholic doctrine.

Matrimony: The sacrament in which a man and woman exchange marital consent before an ordained minister, entering into a relationship which is permanent ("Till death do us part"), exclusive (sexual relations outside the bond of marriage are forbidden), and fruitful (the union must be open to the transmission of human life).

Novena: A nine-day period of prayer, usually for a special intention, based on the nine days spent in prayer by the apostolic community from Ascension Thursday (when Jesus returned to heaven after His several resurrection appearances) until Pentecost Sunday (when the Holy Spirit came upon them and commissioned them as witnesses to the Risen Christ in the world).

Octave: The celebration of a feast for eight days (e.g., Christmas or Easter).

Patristic: Referring to the Fathers of the Church, those saintly and first theologians of the Church whose reflections on Sacred Scripture and explanation of Christian doctrine have formed an indispensable basis for theology ever since. Their era is commonly considered to end in the seventh century in the West and in the eighth century in the East. One of their outstanding contributions was a wedding of Hebraic or biblical thought with Greek philosophy.

Penance: Penance can refer to 1) any act intended to make reparation to Almighty God for past sins; or, 2) that sacrament whereby a Christian confesses his sins to a priest, resolves not to sin again, and receives the absolution of Christ through the ministry of the Church's priest.

Post-conciliar: This expression is generally used in reference to the period after the Second Vatican Council, since its decrees often resulted in attitudes and policies which were different from those held by some Catholics before the Council (particularly as regards non-Catholic Christians or non-Christians).

Prefigurement: The foreshadowing of events or persons from the Old Testament (or Hebrew Scriptures) of events or persons in the New Testament; for example, the sacrifice of Isaac is regarded as giving a type of preparation for the sacrifice of Jesus.

Rite: 1) A religious custom, usage or ceremony; or 2) within the Catholic Church, the various usages by which the sacraments are celebrated in different places and the discipline of that same community. The largest rite is the Latin or Roman Rite, with others such as the Byzantine, Russian, Egyptian, Maronite (Lebanese), etc.

Sacrament of the Sick: In this sacrament, a priest anoints the sick with oil and prays that the person would be restored to physical health, but most especially to spiritual wholeness.

Sanctoral Cycle: In the liturgical year, this term refers to the sequence of feasts and memorials to honor the various saints, whose days can usually be kept only on weekdays and not Sundays.

Sensus plenior: Literally, "the fuller sense" of a scriptural text, so that certain passages of the Bible become clearer in the light of subsequent revelation. Hence, Christians consider the Suffering Servant foretold by Second Isaiah to be realized in Jesus Christ.

Sola Scriptura: Literally, "Scripture alone." This notion was developed by Martin Luther as a principle for theological discussion and development; its adherents argue that Scripture is the only valid source of revelatory data for the formation of doctrine. Neither Catholics nor Eastern Orthodox accept this concept.

Temporal Cycle: This refers to the various seasons (e.g., Advent, Lent) which are celebrated in the course of the liturgical year.

Triduum: A three-day feast or celebration, the most important being the Easter or Paschal Triduum, which includes Holy Thursday (the night of the Last Supper), Good Friday (the day of Christ's death), Holy Saturday/Easter Sunday (Christ's resting in the tomb and resurrection).

Trinitarian: Referring to the Blessed Trinity, the one God in three divine Persons: Father, Son and Holy Spirit.

Vespers: Evening prayers.

Jewish Terms

Bar Mitzvah (Boy)/Bat Mitzvah (Girl): The occasion on which a boy or girl is officially ushered into the adult community of faith. They are expected to assume full religious duties. The boy is called to the Torah reading and is asked to chant a biblical portion of the week. A girl is called to do the same in Conservative and Reform synagogues.

Barakhah: Benediction. Any kind of blessing or prayer of praise before: partaking in food or wine; performing a good deed; kindling the Sabbath lights; or words of thanksgiving to God after seeing lightning or a famous scholar.

Covenant: The call and relationship of God with the people of Israel entailing a body of liturgical and ritual laws that commit both the Jewish individual and the community to keep God's word and commandments in everyday life. *B'rith* in Hebrew.

Emunah: Hebrew word for faith: the acceptance of God's call (amen) and the implementation of God's commands in everyday life, prayer, ritual and theology. To have *Emunah* is to be an active religious person in private life and in the life of the community.

Haggadah: Liturgical text for Passover. It relates the history of God's redemptive action from exile (Egyptian slavery) to the return to the Promised Land and the covenant of the Ten Commandments. The *Haggadah* is read at the *Seder*, the paschal dinner.

Halakhah: Wrongly translated as "law," *Halakhah* is the way God's commandments are implemented in daily life. It is a collection of rules on how to live a life of sacredness expressed in prayers and daily rituals, *Kashroth* and Sabbath observance. It is *Emunah*, faith, in daily practice, a way of religious daily commitment.

Hanukkah (Chanukah): Eight-day celebration, generally in December. Candles are lit on the *menorah* (or *hanukiah)*. One candle is lit at sundown on the first day, two on the second day, etc., for eight consecutive days. This is in commemoration of the victory of Judah

Maccabee over the Greeks (168-165 Before Christian Era [BCE]), and to celebrate the miracle of the tiny jar of oil that kept burning in the Temple for eight days.

Havdalah: Blessing of the wine, candle and spices marking the close of the Sabbath observance.

Hesed: Hebrew word for grace, mercy or loving kindness. In daily prayers Jews recognize the *Hesed* of God in establishing the covenant and the Ten Commandments, rules for sanctity and relationship between human beings.

Hutzpa: The Hebrew word for spiritual arrogance expressed in theological or social matters, but generally for a good cause.

Kabalah: The Jewish mystical tradition and writings.

Kaddish: Special prayer recited at the liturgy on the anniversary of the dead, usually by a close family member. It is a recognition of God's sovereignty and essentially a collection of adjectives praising God's goodness.

Ketubah: A matrimonial document signed between a man and a woman stating both their obligations and rights in the marriage. It is a contract that can be terminated by the Jewish divorce.

Kiddush: Blessing of the wine on the Sabbath and festivals.

Kippah or Yarmulke: A skull cap worn by religious Jews recognizing God's presence and sovereignty. The *Kippah* is used in synagogues, with the exception of some Reform synagogues, who do not follow this custom that seems to have been established in the Middle Ages.

Kosher/Kasher/Kashrut: Food prepared in accordance with traditional Jewish dietary dispositions, including ritual slaughter and separation of meat and dairy products.

Kotel: The western Wailing Wall, last surviving remnant of the Second Temple destroyed in 70 Common Era (CE).

Lag b'Omer: Thirty-third day of the period between Passover and *Shavuoth*, usually around May, associated with the *Bar Kochba* uprising (second century CE) against the Romans. Nowadays it is celebrated with bonfires.

Matzo: Flat, unleavened bread eaten during the Passover holiday, in memory of the haste with which the Hebrews left Egypt since there was no time to allow yeast to rise in baking the bread.

Menorah: Seven-branch candelabrum and a server that stood in the Temple. It is used today for the candles at *Hanukkah.*

Mezuzah: An encased parchment with written Hebrew quotations affixed to the door post of the front door and other doors in Jewish homes.

Midrash: A literary, existential commentary on the Hebrew Bible.

Minyan: Ten Jewish males age thirteen or over required for communal prayer. The Reform synagogues and some Conservative synagogues will count women for the *minyan.*

Mishnah: Compilation of the religious dispositions of the oral tradition completed in the third century of the common era.

Mitzvah: Precept, good deed, religious obligation or duty.

Months of the Year in the Jewish Calendar:
   Tishri: September-October
   Heshvan: October-November
   Kislev: November-December
   Tebet: December-January
   Shebat: January-February
   Adar: February-March
   Nisan: March-April
   Iyar: April-May
   Sivan: May-June
   Tummuz: June-July
   Ab: July-August
   Elul: August-September

Passover/Pesach: Seven-day spring festival commemorating the exodus from Egypt. The first night is marked by a ceremonial meal, *Seder*, at which the *Haggadah* is read.

Purim: Festival commemorating the salvation of the Jews from the hands of Haman, as recorded in the Book of Esther.

Religious Movements in Judaism:

Orthodox Judaism: Orthodox Judaism follows most strictly the full tenets and regulations of the *Halakhah*.

Conservative Judaism: A movement that originated in Germany in the nineteenth century and is active in the United States. The movement seeks to conserve the traditions of Judaism while enlightened about the need for reasonable changes in ritual and observances. Conservatism follows the rules of *Halakhah*, but adapts to present circumstances.

Reform Judaism: It started in nineteenth century Germany, but has achieved its greatest success in the United States. *Halakhah* is considered by the movement as changeable, revocable and adaptable, but also fundamental and not to be tampered with lightly.

Rosh Hashanah: The Jewish new year. Two-day holiday at the beginning of the Hebrew month of *Tishri*, September or October.

Sanhedrin: Supreme Jewish court in Rabbinic times. It does not exist any longer.

Seder: Passover ceremonial meal at which the *Haggadah* is read and special symbolic foods are eaten.

Shabbat: The Sabbath, seventh day of the week, the day of rest.

Shavuoth: Pentecost festival, second of the three annual pilgrim festivals. It commemorates the giving of the Torah and the feast of the harvest and fruits. It occurs around May or June.

Shofar: Ram's horn sounded in the synagogue service on *Rosh Hashanah* and at the conclusion of *Yom Kippur*.

Siddur: The daily prayer book including the prayer services for evening, morning and afternoon.

Simhath Torah: The festival of rejoicing in God's commandments, the last day of *Succoth*, marking the completion in the synagogue of the annual cycle reading of the Torah.

Succah: Temporary booth or tabernacle constructed for the *Succoth* holiday to commemorate the Hebrews' forty years of wandering in the wilderness without permanent dwellings.

Succoth: Seven-day Festival of Tabernacles. It is a tradition that all meals are eaten in the *succah* throughout the week.

Shema: The proclamation of God's unity in the daily liturgy.

Tallith: Four-cornered prayer shawl with fringes, *zizith*, at each corner, used by men during services. It has become the custom in some Reform synagogues for women also to wear a *tallith*.

Talmud: The oral religious law compiled and developed by generations of scholars over a period of several centuries.

Tefilah: The Hebrew word for prayer.

Tefillin: Philacteries, small leather boxes containing parchment passages from Scriptures and affixed on the forehead and arm by observant male Jews during morning prayers.

Tishah b'Av: The ninth day of the Hebrew month of *Ab*, a fast day to mourn the destruction of the First and Second Temples. It has become a custom among some Jews to fast and to mourn the victims of the Holocaust on this day, too.

Torah: Pentateuch, the five books of Moses; also, the handwritten parchment scroll that is read in the synagogue.

Tu Bishevat: Festival of the new year for trees (around July). It is customary to plant trees in Israel and elsewhere and to eat fruits.

Yeshiva: Talmudic school of higher learning.

Yom Kippur: The Day of Atonement, a fast day, the holiest day of the Jewish calendar marks the end of the "ten days of repentance" starting on *Rosh Hashanah*.

Zaddik: Person of outstanding piety and faith.

Zohar: The main text of mystical writings.

Discussion Questions

Doctrine (Chapters One and Two)

1. How can the concept of *shehinah* help a Jewish person understand the Catholic belief in the Holy Trinity?

2. Why is the careful choice of words we use in inter-religious dialogue so important?

3. What is a covenant? Why is God's relationship with Adam and Eve not considered a covenant?

4. What is the significance of God's changing the names of Abram and Sarai?

5. Read Paul's letter to the Romans, chapters nine to eleven. What are some implications for Jews? For the Church?

6. What is meant by *Hesed*, or grace? How are we involved in it?

7. One definition of *Halakhah* is "law." What would be a broader meaning of this term?

8. The Third Commandment instructs us to keep holy the Sabbath, to do no work on this day. Under what circumstances, if any, may this commandment be transgressed?

9. What is the difference between the teaching authority in Judaism and Catholicism?

10. How do the *Mishnah* and the *Midrash* influence biblical interpretation?

11. Explain the Christian understanding of the relationship between the Old and New Testaments.

12. Trace the development of the concept of an afterlife in Judaism.

13. Compare and contrast the concepts of suffering and judgment in Jewish and Christian prayer life.

14. Are the Jews still the Chosen People?

Liturgy (Chapters Three and Four)

15. What is meant by "liturgy"? What are some of its components in Catholic life?

16. What are the differences among Orthodox, Conservative, and Reform Judaism? What are their similarities?

17. How might liturgical reforms be harmful to a particular religion or religious group? Beneficial?

18. What were/are some benefits of using Latin in Catholic liturgy? Hebrew in Jewish worship?

19. What is a Catholic lectionary? How is the current lectionary different from lectionaries prior to Vatican Council II?

20. How are Bible passages presented in the synagogue?

21. What are the similarities and differences in presenting Scripture in Catholicism and Judaism?

22. Why was the first century (A.D.) so important for both Christians and Jews?

23. What aspects of the Catholic liturgy are/were based upon Jewish practices?

24. Describe how the *Kaddish* has changed in meaning. How did Christianity influence this change?

25. How did the Christian rite of Confirmation influence Judaism?

26. Why might Catholicism be more deeply rooted in Judaism than other Christian denominations?

27. In what ways are the celebrations of Passover and the Eucharist alike?

28. Why does the bread used in the Latin Rite resemble *matzo*? Why doesn't the bread used in the Eastern Rites resemble it?

29. How do *Rosh Hashanah* and *Yom Kippur* strengthen one's relationship with God?

30. Why is observing the *Shabbat* so important?

31. Explain the origins of the *menorah.*

32. Identify the segments of the triduum before Easter and explain their significance.

33. Why are Sundays considered feast days in the Christian calendar?

34. Why is there some question about whether or not the Last Supper was a Passover meal? What are some possible explanations for Jesus' sharing of this meal before the actual feast?

The Moral Life (Chapters Five and Six)

35. How do the Ten Commandments fit into the catechesis, or training of Catholics?

36. The Sabbath for both Christians and Jews is a day of rest, not idleness. Explain the difference.

37. How are the sixth and ninth commandments related?

38. How are the seventh and tenth commandments related?

39. What is meant by "biblical morality"?

40. Should Scripture passages on morality be taken literally? Explain.

41. Is marriage a covenant or a contract? Explain.

42. How do Jews and Catholics differ on the question of divorce?

43. Define the Jewish and Catholic positions on abortion.

44. Why is it impossible to state a Jewish position on matters of morality in absolute terms?

45. When can the science of genetics be helpful to a pre-born child? In what ways could it be harmful?

46. In what way is the Jewish family, ideally, a "small Israel"?

47. What is meant by "pluralism"?

48. Discuss why separation of Church and State can be either a positive or negative practice in society.

49. Who first enunciated the "just war" theory? Under what conditions is war justified?

50. In spite of doctrinal differences between Jews and Christians, how can dialogue and cooperative efforts go forward?